IT Production Services

Harris Kern
Richard Schiesser
Mayra Muniz

PRENTICE HALL

Professional Technical Reference

Upper Saddle River, New Jersey 07458

www.phptr.com

Composition: *A. Khedron de León, TIPS Technical Publishing, Inc.*
Cover design director: *Jerry Votta*
Cover design: *Talar Boorujy*
Art director: *Gail Cocker-Bogusz*
Manufacturing manager: *Alexis Heydt-Long*
Manufacturing buyer: *Maura Zaldivar*
Executive editor: *Greg Doench*
Editorial assistant: *Raquel Kaplan*
Marketing manager: *Robin O'Brien*
Full-service production manager: *Robert Kern, TIPS Technical Publishing, Inc.*

Prentice Hall PTR offers excellent discounts on this book when ordered in quantity for bulk purchases or special sales. For more information, please contact: U.S. Corporate and Government Sales, 1-800-382-3419, corpsales@pearsontechgroup.com. For sales outside of the U.S., please contact: International Sales, 1-317-581-3793, international@pearsontechgroup.com

Printed in the United States of America

First printing

ISBN 0-13-065900-2

Pearson Education LTD.
Pearson Education Australia PTY, Limited
Pearson Education Singapore, Pte. Ltd.
Pearson Education North Asia Ltd.
Pearson Education Canada, Ltd.
Pearson Education de Mexico, S.A. de C.V.
Pearson Education–Japan
Pearson Education Malaysia, Pte. Ltd.

We would like to dedicate this book to the following executives who truly know what it takes to build the ideal IT Organization:

Andy Bien, General Manager of IS, Hong Kong Air Cargo
Terminals Limited, Hong Kong

Ajit Kapoor, CTO, Lockheed Martin, Orlando, Florida

Kevin Kryzda, CIO, Martin County, Florida

Daniel Lai, Head of IT, MTR Corporation Limited, Hong Kong

Steven Woodhouse, IT Executive, DITM, Sydney, Australia

Table of Contents

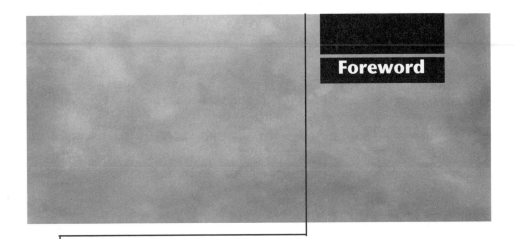

Foreword

During the late 1980s, the trend for Global 2000 companies was to decentralize their Information Technology (IT) organizations. Sun Microsystems, Inc., a Fortune 500 computer hardware manufacturer headquartered in Silicon Valley, California, was no different. Sun had several business units and each one had its own IT department with its own agenda. Each IT department supported its own UNIX computing environment. These decentralized, makeshift IT departments were implementing and supporting their own applications the way they saw fit—usually whatever the customer wanted and whatever made sense for their business, but not necessarily what made sense for the entire company.

Systems Administration support, for example, was typically handled by a group of young engineers who lacked experience managing 24×7 mission-critical data center environments. For these engineers, initiatives such as standards, procedures, and processes lacked importance. It just wasn't on their radar screen. The only thing that mattered to them was slapping systems on the server and connecting them to the network as quickly as possible.

In addition to the decentralized IT units, Sun had a centralized IT department supporting only the company's legacy environment. We were part of that centralized IT data center staff (labeled as "bureaucratic dictators" by our internal customers). Their characterization was accurate.

Our processes were very bureaucratic and slow but very effective for sustaining high availability. Our staff was bred to eat, breathe, and "you know what" high availability. We were not reared to accommodate customers.

By 1990 we knew we had to alter our ways. Our primary goal was to support each business unit and their new client-server technology. We wanted all the production servers that were being designed and managed from broom closets to be housed and supported in our corporate, lily-white data center right alongside the mainframes. The task was a challenging one—nevertheless, in order to change an age-long perception, we had to change the way we provided service to our customers. An impossible mission, right?

Because of our mainframe background, our instinct was to develop an Operations *runbook*[1] type of process. We didn't know where else to begin. We just knew we needed a process. We reasoned that because it worked on the mainframe, it should work on all technologies. A year went by, and we designed a client-server runbook. It was twice the size of the mainframe *runbook* (it's as though we never learned from the past!). Our excuse, however, was all the variables of client-server computing (it wasn't straightforward like mainframe computing). We stuffed everything we could into this big thick document—about 250 pages worth of bureaucracy. We had hundreds of new operational support requirements—here go those bureaucrats again, right? Wrong!

We knew the *runbook* had to be more user friendly, and that we had to promote effective communication practices among the application developers, the IT customers, and the Infrastructure Support staff. These communication improvements were especially critical during the beginning stages of designing, developing, and deploying a new system into production. The importance of staying involved throughout the entire Software Development Life Cycle (SDLC) of each system was abundantly clear to us. We knew that it was just a matter of time before our customers felt overwhelming frustration trying to manage their servers in a 24x7 production environment with a minimum of staff (usually one Systems Administrator and sometimes one Database Administrator). Keeping that in mind, we worked hard to fine-tune our process and devise a plan to market and sell it to our customers (for

---

[1.] *Runbook* is a mainframe process still used today (with mainframe technology only) for data center production support. The procedure provides necessary documentation to effectively support a mission-critical production application.

additional details on marketing and selling IT services, read the book titled *IT Services*). We wanted to be ready to eventually support these systems.

So, here we were, in the late 1980s, with hundreds of servers located in individual business units, supported by dozens of rebellious engineers who wanted absolutely nothing to do with the restrictions and regulations handed to them by the centralized IT staff that governed them throughout the 1960s, 70s, and 80s. They finally got a taste of freedom and complete autonomy when companies began decentralizing their IT functions in the early 90s. In the following few years, however, not adhering to some type of discipline usually cost the department and the corporation dearly. Eventually it became a free-for-all, an ungoverned environment. Unfortunately, life isn't that simple, especially in the world of network computing where some executive at corporate headquarters wants information from Department B's computing systems but is dependant on getting that information from Department A's computing systems. The best example was that of one department's application needing to communicate with another system to attain pertinent information. Not only would the systems not communicate with each other, but fixing the problem would have cost the company millions of dollars. All of this occurred because there were no corporate-wide system standards—something routinely implemented by a centralized or corporate IT group. Each department cared only about their applications and their goals, which were not necessarily goals that would benefit the entire company.

The message was simple. There had to be a "happy medium" between complete decentralization and total oversight by a central department by implementing a sufficient, yet streamlined, set of standards that were to be followed by the satellite business units. It was important that central IT departments prove that they were no longer bureaucratic, and that the satellite groups could support their systems competently while providing a better level of service.

Because of the political atmosphere, the entire company branded the mainframe staff (us) as dinosaurs. Our venture was made more difficult because of the many people issues involved. There were so many skeptics in the company, beginning with our executive management team. They repeatedly denied us the use of processes, always pontificating "no mainframe disciplines!" They felt their only choice was to turn their backs on us, so they refused to support our efforts at designing and implementing these processes. They had to side with the majority—it was the politically correct thing to do. We had no choice but to pursue our efforts to design the Production Acceptance process under the table—on our own time. We truly had no choice, if we wanted to be successful.

Customers and executive management consistently bet against us. We were determined to stay focused regardless of the obstacles. It took us three years to design, implement, streamline, market and sell the process to Sun's internal customers. Why did it take three years? Because we didn't know what we were designing—we were breaking new ground. We just knew that if we didn't have some type of process to manage the hundreds of servers that were being designed from every part of the globe, supporting them would be complete chaos.

In 1991, we successfully designed and implemented the first UNIX Production Acceptance (UPA) process. This gave way to its successor, the Client-Server Production Acceptance (CSPA) process, and that completed our goal of designing a process to cost-effectively support all of Sun Microsystem's mission-critical, client-server systems.

We knew if we could win the hearts and minds of a single key customer, then executive management would have no choice but to listen. So we went on an all-out marketing blitz to try and find a friend—a friendly customer with whom we could pilot our process. We found our first client—a "friendly" customer in marketing (yes we actually found one) to help us streamline this beast. We wanted to ensure success by cost-effectively providing infrastructure support to one of their non-mission-critical applications. We knew we had to ease up on the bureaucracy and stop thinking like "mainframers." As we piloted their application, many of our original restrictions were lifted—we truly made things effortless.

As a result, we improved productivity time for their development staff. This, in turn, allowed them to focus solely on Applications Development functions. In many of these decentralized IT organizations, Applications Development personnel would perform their own Systems Administration functions. In most instances, even the most basic Systems Administration function, such as performing daily backups, was bypassed.

Once the customers were engaged in our new user-friendly process, they could see we had changed our bureaucratic ways. We realized we were definitely on our way to rewriting IT history. Our approach was basic, and we articulated it to our customers: We will oversee your department's Systems Administration function and you can focus your energies on designing and developing new systems. We convinced them that it was always more exciting to play with the latest and greatest technology then it was to perform daily backups.

Time and suffering became our greatest ally. Several departments were already feeling some distress from having to perform their own Systems Administration functions. Performing daily backups is a dismal and tedious Systems Administration function. In our centralized IT organization, we had a function to ensure:

- Daily, weekly, monthly, quarterly, and yearly backups
- Data integrity (ability to read the tape)
- Offsite storage for Disaster Recovery purposes
- Testing of the restore and recovery procedures

This function was routine for us because it is one of our core competencies. Our customers had a difficult time with this function because it was certainly not one of their core competencies and they did not have a dedicated resource. In the course of performing those backups, they were losing data from poor tape handling, wasting time and precious resources to restore data when needed. Obviously, the more agonizing pain they felt, the easier it would be to sell our Production Acceptance process—and we sold it! And, we rewrote the IT history books!

We worked hard, fought long, and learned much as we successfully implemented our first CSPA process at Sun Microsystems many years ago. We have since refined this process and implemented it at many other major companies. In this book, we relate many of our experiences and successes at these companies in helping their IT infrastructures truly become a competitive advantage to the business.

Although we speak of the drama we went through to reach this point in our history, we must admit this scenario of decentralized and centralized organizations working together in a disorderly fashion still exists today. The problem, however, goes far beyond decentralized and centralized IT organizations. In IT environments where Applications Development and Infrastructure Support groups report to one centralized organization, the problem is just as prevalent. The Production Acceptance process and the lack of a newly designed Production Control function is by far the Number One process and organizational issue in IT today.

This then became the basis for our unwavering belief in the importance of a Production Services (PS) function. We knew that such a function, coupled with a Production Acceptance process, could address many of the shortcomings that infrastructures were experiencing as they struggled to transition to a client-server environment and are still incurring in network computing environments today.

—The Authors

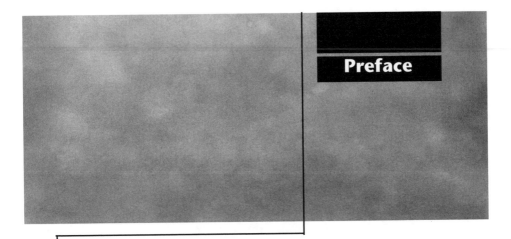

Preface

What ever happened to that sacred production environment where newly developed systems went through a stringent interrogation process before they were allowed entrance? It took an act of God, and then some, to bypass the thorough and intricate mainframe process to rush a new system onto the raised floor of the data center. What made the mainframe environment so successful were the *commitments* of the people and the robustness of the processes. Even though the tedious and complex operations of mainframes eventually led to their downfall, they built the foundation for what could become robust infrastructures of the future. In the quest to meet unreasonable budgets and impossible schedules at the cost of quality, however, today's newly developed systems are frequently thrown over the wall and slam-dunked into production. Information Technology (IT) went from an environment that was extremely strict, structured, and disciplined to one that is now lenient, unorganized, and unrestricted.

In this book, we're introducing a newly designed Production Services function, which addresses the needs of multiple departments within IT, including Applications Development and Computer Operations. Just as important, this function addresses the needs of the customers of all newly developed IT systems being transitioned from Applications Development into production. We also highlight the Production Acceptance process used for every new system moving from the development phase into a production mode. Production Acceptance is the most critical process for addressing:

- Infrastructure Support requirements
- Poor communication between IT and its customers regarding newly developed systems
- Lack of communication between Applications Development and Production/Infrastructure Support
- Support roles and responsibilities
- Training and system documentation
- Customer's expectations (service levels)

One of the main reasons that 70 percent of all IT organizations today are still labeled as cost centers, and are failing miserably, is because of their infrastructures. Infrastructures are in horrible shape, as we will exhibit in our IT assessment data. We will share with you the data compiled from over 200 IT assessments from Fortune 500 and Global 2000 companies, but more importantly we will share how this new Production Services function resolves many of those issues. We will show you how to design and change your infrastructure into a world-class Information Technology Service Provider (ITSP), not just a high-priced support center.

Let's not forget the organization structure, which is the number one problem in IT today. We discuss the top organizational issues affecting the staff and executive management and how our ten commandments can help design a cost-effective and efficient IT organization.

To round it out, we will provide documented case studies of our experiences with several major companies across the country. These studies discuss the strengths and weaknesses of each company's infrastructure environment and the lessons learned in addressing their Production Services issues. Finally, we will provide answers to some of the most frequently asked questions relating to IT infrastructures.

This book is intended for CIOs, CTOs, management staff, Infrastructure Services staff, and Architects responsible for building a competetive advantage to business IT organizations.

Acknowledgements

Harris Kern

I would like to thank the following people who have made the Harris Kern Enterprise Computing Institute (HKECI) the force that it is today:

- Michael Hawkins; co-author of *Data Warehousing, High Availability*
- Howie Lyke; author of *IT Automation*
- Rich Schiesser; author of *IT Systems Management* and co-author of *IT Production Services*
- Tony Tardugno; co-author of *IT Services*
- Robert Matthews; co-author of *IT Services*
- Tom Dipasquale; co-author of *IT Services*
- Guy Nemiro; co-author of *IT Organization*
- Marc Hamilton; author of *Software Development*
- Stuart Galup; co-author of *IT Organization*
- Cooper Smith; author of *Technology Strategies* and co-author of *Web-Based Infrastructures*
- Alex Nghiem; author of *IT Web Services*
- Jane Carbone; author of *IT Architecture Toolkit*
- Sanmay Mukhopadhyay; co-author of *Web-Based Infrastructures*
- Ken Moskowitz; co-author of *Managing IT as an Investment*
- Mayra Muniz; co-author of *IT Production Services*
- Gary Walker; author of *IT Problem Management*
- Dean Lane, author of *CIO Wisdom*
- And last but not least, my friend Greg Doench, Executive Editor at PTR/Prentice Hall

Without these individuals the series would just be another set of books. Thank you all from the bottom of my heart!

Rich Schiesser

I want to thank Harris Kern for his encouragement, his clarity, and his support in communicating his wealth of experiences that pertain to the topics in this book. His willingness to share his knowledge of what makes for an ideal IT environment with others is what makes so much of this book possible. I would like to thank Mayra Muniz for her close attention to detail, for her help with the overall organization and flow of our work, and for having the patience of Job. Finally and most importantly, I want to thank the person who motivates me the most, who criticizes me the least, and who consoles me the best—my lovely wife, Ann.

Mayra Muniz

I would like to thank my husband for his undying love and support, and for the unconditional love and support I receive from my loving kids, Chade and Christian, and my mother Lillian. I'd also like to thank Greg Doench and his wonderful staff, who have also contributed to Harris Kern's Enterprise Computing Institute, helping us make it the success it is today.

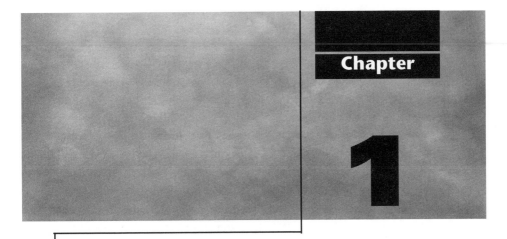

Chapter

1

Background

Introduction

This chapter traces the evolutionary development of the data center in relation to the Production Control function of the mainframe environment over the past 30 years and describes how this critical area met its temporary demise in the late 1980s. The chapter concludes with a brief discussion of how Production Control is now evolving itself into a more relevant Production Services function and is being put to use in world class infrastructures.

The Data Center Heritage

We will never forget our early years reared in a mainframe-based data center, when being promoted into a computer operator position, which usually started out on graveyard shift, meant executing and monitoring the mission-critical batch cycles. We manually mounted and unloaded hundreds of tapes a night, treating each backup as if it were a bar of gold. Our supervisor (bless his heart) was like a drill sergeant, always scaring the heck out of us to ensure that we would never mislabel or write over the wrong tape. This is what the data center stood for—discipline was a way of life in the world of data processing.

An integral part of the data center's success was something we referred to as Reliability, Availability, and Serviceability (RAS). RAS was always priority number one in the 1970s and early 1980s for the data center support staff. RAS was more than just an acronym. It was a way of ensuring continuous customer access to their computing environment by establishing and adhering to processes and implementing global standards. Processes and key functions used to support mission-critical applications were entrenched in the infrastructure to ensure RAS. Table 1–1 lists only some of the functions, key processes, and initiatives that ensured RAS.

Table 1–1 Ingredients for RAS

Function	Description
Tape Librarian	Ensured proper backups, data integrity, offsite retention, audits, etc.
Production Control	Process ownership, standards compliance, documentation, production gatekeepers, etc.
Metrics	IT services (i.e. response times, availability, etc.,) must be measured to more effectively manage the environment.
Disaster Recovery	A documented process with rehearsed drills (usually performed quarterly) at an offsite location.
Pre-Production Environment	All systems go through rigorous testing before being turned over to production.
System Management Disciplines	Change Management, Problem Management, Capacity Planning, etc.

Unfortunately, during the late 1980s and into the 1990s, these Production Control functions and processes were put on a back burner so companies could focus on technology. New-wave propeller heads tried to bury these disciplines because they evolved from the mainframe era. The perception was that centralized or corporate IT somehow symbolized the slow and bureaucratic. Times have changed and the focus is now back on providing high availability, focusing on customer service, and being cost effective. It is a tall set of orders, but it is no longer an option—it is a necessity.

To accomplish this arduous mission, the first priority would have to be for the Infrastructure Services Oganization to work closely with the Applications Development staff early on in the design and deployment of new applications, systems, and/or technology. To do so would require a process designed, developed, and owned by the Infrastructure Services Organization that was accountable for the mission. It would require a process that ensured focusing on customer service, continuous communications between Applications Development and Infrastructure Support functions, and high availability—from the beginning of the system design phase straight through production deployment.

Regrettably, a common factor within IT today is the lack of a process for the infrastructure organization to manage such responsibilities. Every IT person knows what Quality Assurance (QA) is and the key role it plays in developing new systems or revising existing applications, regardless of the technology (mainframe, client-server, Web, network computing, etc.). QA is a very critical function that has been around for decades. Its primary purpose was to manage the migration of new code into production. In the 21st century, QA is still a requirement for Applications Development and has now also become a requirement for Production Services.

Production QA

The first question one might ask is: Why in the world would you want to introduce another QA function and introduce the potential for more bureaucracy? Well, in today's fast-paced network computing environment, everyone in IT has no choice but to work harder and put in longer hours just to keep up with customer demands, fewer resources, and rapidly evolving technology. Customers want everything "yesterday," including the deployment of systems the moment the Applications Development or executive management staff says they are ready. In most companies, the Infrastructure Support staff is not involved in the early stages of the SDLC, when many of the infrastructure requirements need to be identified and addressed. The Infrastructure Support group often is not allowed involvement in the SDLC until it is time to go live. Unfortunately, once the system is labeled "production ready," the burden to maintain high availability falls squarely on the shoulders of the Infrastructure Support staff. If the support staff does not comply, they are made to look like the bad guys. Compliance by the Infrastructure Support staff is usually not required. After all, the company is dependent on this new system and it must go live on a certain date regardless of the consequences—how many times have we heard that line in IT? There's never enough time to test and thoroughly QA a system, however there is always ample time to revise it, if necessary. The bottom line is that introducing a production QA function, which focuses on infrastructure requirements to both Applications Development and to the production Infrastructure Support staff would be the ticket to ensuring and preserving RAS in the data center and everything it stands for.

Production Control

The Production Control organization was established in the early 1970s to provide a QA function for the legacy environment. Its functions were to:

- Provide second level production support
- Participate in the Disaster Recovery process/drills
- Reject new applications or major revisions to applications prior to thorough testing, staff training, and documentation
- Breed technical resources
- Maintain scheduling requirements
- Provide centralized ownership/accountability for key processes (i.e., Change Management, Storage Management, etc.)
- Maintain system management tools
- Assist senior systems programmers in the installation, support, and documentation thereof
- Provide training to other groups within IT on newly installed system management tools

The staff was best known for their hard-nosed, dictator attitude. They were branded the "gatekeepers" to the mission-critical data center environment.

Why Bring This Function Back?

We've been asked this question hundreds of times from every part of this country. The answer is always: *IT needs to ensure a high level of customer service and preserve RAS.* That response is based on actual data from our IT planning and development workshops (see Chapter 3). The list was appalling, but was it shocking? No, primarily because IT organizations try to effectively manage the infrastructure on a part-time basis—it's never a priority. Deploying new systems and technology is always a priority. Ensuring high customer satisfaction, however, *must* also be a top priority.

Production Control vs. Applications Development

When IT began to ignore the Production Control organization, it subsequently disregarded and discarded processes and people issues. One of the primary reasons for writing this book was to showcase the results from dozens of IT planning and development workshops. After facilitating these workshops with Fortune 500 and Global 2000 companies, it became apparent that organization, people, and process focus was lacking throughout most IT organizations.

One of the primary functions of the Production Control group was to accept or decline new systems/applications from the Applications Development department into what the Infrastructure Support staff considered the "sacred" production environment. Its job was to ensure high availability by not contaminating the production environment with poorly developed, improperly tested, and poorly documented systems. On the other hand, Applications Development's charter is to design, develop, and deploy a system into production as quickly as possible.

Two Worlds Clash

Nothing entered the holy temple (the data center) until the proper documentation was provided, the appropriate staff was trained, and the application went through a very thorough QA process. The Production Control staff had as much power to prevent a new system from being deployed into production as the Applications Development staff had for bypassing the normal process to expedite a system into production. There was no bargaining. It was Production Control's way or the system would end up in the department's broom closet—not supported by the data center/Infrastructure Support staff. You can imagine the friction this caused.

This dictatorial type of behavior by the Production Control staff lasted throughout the 1970s and midway through the 1980s. The mainframe function was one-sided in favor of the Production Control group. It was not until the late 1980s and throughout the 1990s, as most companies transitioned to a decentralized client-server computing environment, that they did away with the Production Control function; with it went the production QA function altogether. Along with production QA went RAS. RAS became a thing of the past.

Some companies tried to keep this organization intact by changing the function dramatically. The perception was that Production Control was bureaucratic and slow. As technologies were evolving at a torrid pace in the late 1980s and through the 1990s, this perception became a reality throughout IT. It sometimes took several weeks to put a system into production. The intent was good, but it really slowed down the deployment of new systems, which in turn angered the user community. The bureaucracy was unbearable. We discovered that a happy medium is absolutely necessary between bureaucratic legacy environments and today's networked, heterogeneous world.

In the 1990s, this same centralized Production Control staff would not dare say no to new systems or applications being deployed into a production environment, regardless of whether or not anyone followed a process or procedure. Its support responsibilities were pretty much contained to mainframe applications. Because of their bureaucratic process and dictatorial behavior, the newer client-server technologies were off limits. There were a few companies that still had centralized Production Control staffs supporting all applications, but their responsibilities were very limited. If, for whatever reason, they declined (i.e., through poor Operations documentation) to accept the new system into the corporate production environment, the customer/owner of the new system would construct their own systems—even if it meant installing the server in their office. Once the system was declined by Production Control, the customer had no choice but to install the server wherever possible because they still had a business to support.

Once a system went into production status, it became certified production-ready and was consequently located in the corporate or regional data center; the buck then stopped with Production Control. If the system was unstable (unable to maintain 99.9 percent uptime) there was no one at whom to point fingers but themselves. Production Control's failure during the legacy environment, and even in today's network world, was determined by postponement of communication or lack thereof. Production Control waited until the application was complete before they started communicating with Applications Development staff regarding their system requirements. There was very little communication between Applications Development and the entire Infrastructure Support staff—*especially* Production Control.

Evolving Production Control into Production Services

During the 1990s, many shops began hosting mission-critical applications on client-server platforms rather than mainframes. This trend further reduced the role of Production Control that had its roots in the mainframe environment. Production Control and their mainframe disciplines were not involved in the early design of these new client-server systems, and were never involved in all of the appropriate pre-production activities. Systems were literally thrown over the wall into production. Production Control was never involved until Applications Development said their systems were ready. Generally nine times out of 10, the systems were not ready for production.

Thirty years later we are still defining key elements in our methodologies to build the ideal IT organization (see Chapter 4) and not to discard any of the mainframe disciplines (processes and standards). Today's IT shops should embrace these system management disciplines and, in the process, re-engineer and customize each one as well as remove any bureaucracy associated with the legacy world.

In applying this approach to the Production Control area, we propose replacing it with a more refined, up-to-date version of it that we call *Production Services*. This new function includes many of the features of the mainframe-oriented Production Control, but with the added flexibility to manage the more dynamic nature of client-server and even Web-enabled applications. The cornerstone of Production Services is a Production Acceptance process that builds into a production deployment all of the infrastructure areas that are needed to ensure production readiness. These areas include (among others):

- The Help Desk
- Capacity Planning

- Storage Management
- Business continuity
- Desktop Services
- Systems Administration
- Database Administration
- Networking

The Production Services function and the Production Acceptance process will be described in detail in subsequent chapters.

Summary

This chapter began by describing the critical roles of the Production Control function in the 1970s and early 1980s for mainframe environments. We then discussed how the proliferation of client-server applications gradually reduced the use of mainframes in the late 1980s—and later Web-enabled systems during the 1990s. These events diminished the role of Production Control, resulting in a fair degree of instability for newly deployed applications. Our answer to this problem is a more refined, modern version of this function we call Production Services. This chapter concluded with a brief introduction to this new infrastructure discipline.

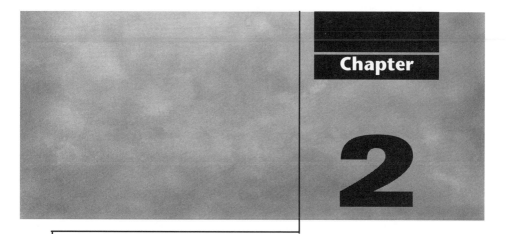

2

Ten Commandments for Building the Ideal IT Environment

Introduction

This chapter describes the top IT issues and challenges facing CIOs today, and serves as the foundation for our 10 commandments for building the ideal IT environment. We present the top issues we have identified from our workshops, assessments, and consulting activities with hundreds of major IT organizations in both the private and public sectors worldwide. We then discuss the various solutions we developed to address these diverse issues. These solutions all center, in priority order, on organization, people, process, and technology. Finally, we list and explain our ten commandments for building the ideal IT environment.

Top IT Issues and Challenges

After studying over 200 Fortune 500 and Global 2000 companies, we have compiled a list of the top issues and challenges plaguing IT executives. It is no wonder IT is still considered a cost center by its business counterpart in 70 percent of the global 2000 companies.

The following are frequently asked questions provided to us from IT professionals. The questions are evidence of their underlying issues, which differ from those highlighted in Chapter 3, in that those issues are related to the infrastructure whereas these pertain to the entire IT organization and the enterprise that it serves.

- How can CIOs lead, educate, and partner with CEOs and the executive management team?
- How can IT ask the right questions and jointly specify project requirements?
- How do IT executives market and enhance their value to the enterprise?
- How can IT prevent business units from throwing project requirements over the transom (often as solutions masquerading as requirements)?
- How can IT stop purchasing technology for technology's sake and align itself with business objectives?
- How can IT stop the mistrust and develop credibility?
- How can IT change the mindset that IT works for IT's sake into a customer-centric culture?
- How can IT jointly develop business cases used to determine priority?
- IT can do a good job of following orders, but how do they change the culture to one that has creative solutions?
- How can IT get its business partners to communicate IT's value to the enterprise?

Traditionally annual IT strategic planning is typically a static, yet discrete, process. It takes considerable time (often four to six months) to produce a large, static document that details projects and timetables from a technology versus business viewpoint.

- How do we change this process into one that is more tightly integrated with the business?

- How can IT nurture the staff to achieve exceptional productivity and job satisfaction?

- How can IT do a better job of thinking strategically and being more proactive instead of always being in a reactive mode in their production environment?

- What are the minimum yet sufficient processes required to build the ideal IT organization?

- How can IT maintain centralized control for standards, processes, and architectures?

- Communication is atrocious, especially between Applications Development and Infrastructure Support. How can IT get these people to play together?

- Systems are being slam-dunked into production—how can IT ensure a smooth transition from development to production?

- How can IT become more cost efficient?

- How can IT design an infrastructure that is a competitive advantage? What are the top issues/obstacles to overcome when building the proper infrastructure?

- How can IT stop working in silos and start becoming a team with synergy?

- How can IT change the perception that centralized IT is bureaucratic to one of adaptability?

- How can IT change from related communication (isolated) to developing key relationships?

- The customers of IT services currently manage their vendors. How can IT overturn this process so vendors are managed by IT?

- How can IT build for efficiency and effectiveness, and architect for growth and business alignment?

To look at these at a higher level, note the following top six IT issues:

1. IT is not aligned with the business
   - Support/cost center mindset versus customer solutions provider mindset
   - Services catalog is missing or not well defined

2. Communication is ineffective
   - Between IT and the business
   - Within IT
   - Between IT and vendors/external service providers

3. I've cut as much as I can cut. It's still not enough. Now what?
   - How do I make what I have work?
   - How do I get what I thought I was going to get out of it when I bought it?

4. Organizational problems
   - Silos
   - Missing key functions
   - Technology-centric and/or functional-centric versus services-centric

5. Process problems
   - Missing or ineffective processes
   - Bureaucratic processes
   - Minimum but barely sufficient processes

6. People problems
   - Day-to-day behaviors are not aligned with or do not support organizational objectives
   - "Genetic makeup" of technology workers
   - New ways to lead and manage are required if you want the behavior to change
   - Roles and responsibilities are not clearly defined for networked computing
   - Skill development, knowledge transferring, and mentoring are nonexistent

It is no surprise to us, and probably no surprise to you, that almost half of the issues implicate the infrastructure! No wonder IT is still considered a cost center and it is not aligned with the business.

The Infrastructure

Historically, companies supporting networked computing environments share a common problem when structuring their organization in an attempt to effectively manage their environment. As a general rule, large investments are being made to develop and deploy systems as quickly as possible. Because the application is the human interface to the end-user, most of the effort, investments, and focus are placed there, leaving very little attention on the underlying people/process issues specific to the operational infrastructure. An unstable technical infrastructure is the result of this lack of attention.

The New IT Challenge

Building the ideal IT infrastructure to support a mission-critical production environment is by far the number one challenge in IT today because the issues are overwhelming. How can an organization eliminate these problems in a timely and cost-effective manner? These enterprises are bleeding profusely because of the many years of procrastination and neglect of these infrastructure issues. Merely focusing on new system development and technology has finally taken its toll and is costing companies millions. Executives understand the issues and know that it will take years and a whole lot of time and money to stop the hemorrhaging. The issues are common and widespread throughout all industries (i.e., telecommunications, manufacturing, entertainment and media, etc.). No one is excluded.

Other challenges for today's executives are:

- Satisfying rapid ramp-up and/or multi-location infrastructure requirements
- Gaining and maintaining market advantage with leading edge technology and services
- Reducing IT support costs/improving cost controls

This is a daunting list of initiatives and, as in all IT shops, we guarantee that it is associated with aggressive schedules. To address many of these challenges executives are looking outside their confines for answers. They are looking to replace or outsource inadequate, underperforming IT Operations. They are seeking guidance from Infrastructure Services providers for quick solutions. A word of caution to these executives: Do you think these service providers—many of which came out of the cupboards overnight—have their acts together?

Executives, please heed this warning: If you outsource trash, you will receive twice the trash in return. This, of course, means twice as many headaches. You will have to manage two dumpsites. You will still have to deal with your customers in addition to dealing with the vendor that stores your trash.

A Radical Approach

IT infrastructure executives' only choice is to alter their current direction or abandon ship. They need to change the way they currently provide services to their internal customers. IT infrastructures have been designated as a cost center for too many years. It is time to manage IT as an investment, not as overhead.

IT infrastructure organizations need to start transitioning themselves from an IT support shop to an IT Service Provider (ITSP)! Your IT infrastructure organization needs to transition itself into becoming a business. It can no longer be labeled just a support organization. It is no longer a question of whether to do it or not—executives need to address this issue as soon as possible (ASAP) and stop procrastinating. Today's enterprises need to:

- Rapidly transition the traditional back-office IT infrastructure function into a full-scale development and support environment
- Architect and implement the complex networks and hosting environments that new applications require
- Satisfy demanding new service levels
- Change the infrastructure group's mindset to that of a competitive service provider. It can no longer be labeled "support"
- Address the organization structure, people, and process issues

- Design a services portfolio and a process portfolio
- Design a communications plan internal to IT and external to clients
- Train staff in soft skills
- Address IT's cost and value—benchmarking and resource allocation
- Convert IT's mindset and behaviors from monopolistic operation to that of a competitive operation

The only way to turn this around is by effectively using people and technology. This approach is radical, but infrastructures today are a huge overhead, draining corporate profits. This ineffective use of people and technology is not only a waste but it also makes for some unhappy corporate customers who are not as productive as they could be. In addition, they're not getting the services they require.

IT executives need to finally invest the time and resources into building an infrastructure that becomes a *competitive advantage* for the business.

Laying The Foundation

For infrastructures to change their current mode of operation and transition to becoming an internal service provider, they need to lay down the foundation with the following fundamental elements:

- A comprehensive *infrastructure development and support methodology*
- Necessary system management *tools*
- Enterprise-wide, system management *processes*
- Documented *architecture*
- Addressing the *people* issues
- Appropriate *organizational structure*

IT executives need to finally invest the time and resources into building a world class infrastructure where they manage IT as an investment in the corporation rather than a cost center.

Infrastructure Development and Support Methodology

The infrastructure development and support methodology, which is a fancy title for a Production Acceptance process (see Chapter 5), ensures the quality and reliability of your service delivery platform. Your service delivery platform is typically a server with one application or multiple applications.

Production Acceptance is a methodology that engages applications and systems development and operational support functions early on to effectively deploy and support all new systems.

The Production Acceptance process is required to transfer new applications (or major revisions) and systems into production or launch new projects. Without this process, the result will be an unstable production environment with poor reliability and availability.

Production Acceptance complements Applications Development by ensuring that all operational requirements are accounted for in the architecture, design, development, and deployment of new systems. The Production Acceptance process provides a checklist of requirements needed by operational groups to support a system installation for deployment into production. This process also insures that the proper infrastructure (i.e., network bandwidth, system management tools, facilities requirements, etc.) is ready for this new system. This process is required for introducing into production each new or major revision to an application, system, or project. Without an enterprise-wide Production Acceptance process, the result will be poor RAS. For more information on this process, refer to Chapter 5.

This methodology also becomes your production QA initiative for ensuring high availability, security, and customer service. This QA function should reside within a Production Services group (see Chapter 4) designed, implemented, and maintained by second-level support personnel. The process will spell out everyone's roles and responsibilities for implementing and supporting mission-critical production systems. Production Acceptance is a process used to effectively deploy and support mission-critical applications and ensure that customers get the same reliability, availability, and security that they did with their mainframe applications. Production Acceptance is the best way of maintaining and improving IT and customer dialogue, as well as providing a QA process for systems support and development. Just as client-server has revolutionized the computing paradigm, the Production Acceptance process is our contribution to a new age of IT customer relations through personalized communications.

Tools and Technology

Tools and technology enable you to quickly and efficiently launch and support applications. Many of these tools need to be designed and developed by your infrastructure organization. The typical toolset includes, but is not limited to:

- Back-Office Tools (customer satisfaction surveys, service tracking, etc.)

  As you are providing services to your customer, you will need to design and implement some type of service-tracking system that allows you to track all customer requests for services. Once these services have been completed, you need to gauge how effective your organization was in providing those services. A simple point-and-click solution must be designed to gauge customer satisfaction for all services provided by IT. Many IT shops have a tendency to measure a percentage of services provided or do it on monthly or quarterly intervals. All it takes is one unhappy customer to escalate a problem or issue to the wrong executive.

- Systems Management Solutions

  Enterprise-wide system management solutions must be fully implemented and customized to automate as much of the production environment as possible in an effort to be cost effective.

- Charge Back Methodology

  Once your organization has completed these services and you've got some happy customers, it's time to give them a bill for services rendered.

Processes

Minimum, Yet Sufficient, Processes

This new service provider model must have the minimum, yet sufficient, set of processes to manage the mission-critical production environment. The minimum set of processes to cost-effectively manage for success are Production Acceptance, Change Management, and Problem Management.

Documented Procedures

Procedures must be documented and maintained by your data center Operations staff.

Service Level Agreements (SLAs)

Expectations between IT and its customers must be clearly documented, communicated, and managed. IT must also develop internal SLAs to improve the communication and expectations between development and support groups.

Managed Communications

To improve communications, you need to start with a Production Acceptance process. The primary function of Production Acceptance is to define and coordinate everyone's roles and responsibilities and ensure that communication is continuously practiced.

Metrics

We have been saying it for years: How can personnel cost-effectively manage their environment unless they know the numbers? Whether it's measuring customer satisfaction, server availability, etc., performance metrics are a key factor in transitioning your organization into a service provider.

Architecture

Architecture Standards

You need a vision and plan along with some well documented hardware and software enterprise-wide standards.

The People

Clearly Defined Roles and Responsibilities

In today's networked world, there are very few clear lines of demarcation identifying everyone's roles and responsibilities. Duplication of effort and dropped support responsibilities run rampant throughout IT.

You still need job descriptions, but you will also need to clearly define everyone's roles and responsibilities for each production application. Documenting roles and responsibilities one time and putting them on a shelf will not work. Each mission-critical application housed in a production environment must have its support and development staff clearly defined. This should be done via the Production Acceptance process.

Inscribed Career Development Path

A clearly defined career path for technical staff and management is critical to maintaining morale, keeping turnover low, and breeding internal resources.

Training

Continuous education, which includes technology/process certifications can also be a morale booster and lead to career development.

Behaviors

In today's economic climate, much is being discussed, written, and applied regarding the IT value chain and the best practices in IT management, focusing on three fundamental dimensions: the ever-elusive People-Process-Technology trilogy. It is imperative, however, that IT executives look deeper into their organization to identify, understand, and address the true source of their successes and failures—the collective behavior of their people.

The Organization

Service Orientation

Technology-centric and/or functional-centric versus services-centric. For an organization to excel it *must* be services-centric first and then focus on technology and functionality.

Three-Tier Support Model

The proper three-tier support structure must be in place to quickly and efficiently resolve problems.

Process Ownership and Accountability

There needs to be a centralized organization accountable for enterprise-wide system management processes. We refer to this function as Production Services (see Chapter 4). The Production Services organization should *always* be structured at the enterprise level of the Enterprise Infrastructure Services Organization.

In order for IT to be a successful partner with its business counterparts these fundamental elements need to be addressed ASAP. The first step is to define the ideal IT environment.

Our definition of the *ideal IT environment* is one that is designed to exceed the enterprise's strategic goals while nurturing the *individual* to achieve exceptional *productivity* and *job satisfaction*. The following signs are an indication of such an environment:

- Educated and committed enterprise executive management
- Complete alignment with business goals and objectives
- Strategic decisions that accommodate a rapidly changing dynamic business environment
- Cost effectiveness
- Common architecture (i.e., processes, tools, standards, etc.)
- Individuals blossoming instead of being buried in a bureaucracy
- A culture where honesty, mutual respect, creativity, and job satisfaction flourish

When designing the ideal IT organization, a critical piece of the equation is establishing the right methodologies, or what we refer to as the *Ten Commandments for building the ideal IT organization*. As depicted in the previous list, most of the issues are not related to technology. When designing this environment, the focus should be on:

- Organization
- People
- Processes
- Technology

Just like most people abide by a set of commandments in our everyday life, the same holds true for IT staff responsible for establishing the ideal IT environment. IT organizations need a game plan or what we commonly refer to as a "playbook" when building the proper computing environment. In this chapter, we provide you with those guidelines—the Ten Commandments.

The Ten Commandments

I. Thou shalt organize to focus on mission critical.

The first step is to properly structure the organization to support a heterogeneous computing environment, which is the most important and critical aspect of implementing a cost-effective infrastructure. If the organization is structured properly, processes can flourish and *high availability* will be attainable.

The secret to properly structuring the organization is to focus on mission-critical systems rather than the technology. Split your Infrastructure Services Organization into two parts—mission critical and non-mission critical. It's up to you and your customers to determine what is mission critical and what is not. See Table 2–1 for examples.

Define the scope of production. Define which system is truly mission critical to the company. How much revenue will be lost if that system is down for a variable number of minutes? Don't proclaim everything as mission critical. Be frugal. If you try to take on the world, you will surely fail. So many companies structure their organization to support a particular technology. Whether you run your business on NT, UNIX, or another operating system, *never* structure to focus on a particular technology. This is one of the most common mistakes in IT. IT should always structure to support RAS while focusing on customer service. RAS was, and still should be, synonymous with the concept of mission critical. With RAS and customer service as the focus of your organization, the entire computing environment will flourish.

Table 2–1   Examples of Mission-Critical vs. Non-Mission-Critical Systems

Mission-Critical	Non-Mission-Critical
Payroll systems	Marketing systems
WAN	Training
Manufacturing systems	Reporting systems
Data Center production servers	Office systems

II. Thou shalt partner and align with the business.

IT needs to be organized to respond rapidly to the needs of individual business groups. This requires a planning process tightly integrated with each of the business groups and an enterprise-wide vision within which all of these needs can be met. This can only be accomplished by establishing working relationships at individual and group levels with all business partners.

Business teams, including IT as a business, work together. Besides enterprise infrastructure, there is no such thing as an IT project. Whether IT is responsible for 10 percent of the tasks or 90 percent, IT is merely a member of a business team led by a business project champion. All projects require business unit champions and business project champions.

All members of this business team are scheduled with accountabilities and deliverables. Priorities are determined through jointly developed business cases. All projects are required to build a business case—a technology case is not sufficient. All business cases are required to discuss alignment of objectives with enterprise objectives. IT is inseparable from the business and requires complete alignment with business goals.

Alignment with the business needs to be more than a strategic plan or a written set of operating principles. The technology organization needs to be set up in a way that allows business alignment to flow as a natural consequence of the way the job is done.

In order to flexibly align with the business, IT needs to be able to react both functionally (e.g., deep technical skills) and geographically (e.g., globally, regionally, or locally) to business imperatives. The solution is a matrix organization that combines shared services with personnel dedicated to business units at the global, regional, and local levels. This can accommodate any enterprise needs by strengthening or weakening dotted lines and/or standards/guidelines.

The only way to align with the business is to become a part of the business. Dedicated Applications Development staff—physically sitting with the business, having its operational priorities set by the business, participating in business operations and strategy, and having its budget overseen by its line of business—forces technology to be aligned with the business. The key to the matrix is that these groups, for all practical purposes reporting to the line of business, are reporting on a straight line to technology and on a very strong dotted line to the business (see Figure 2–1). This unit is a part of the business but ultimately reports to technology. The management principles to be followed are a strict adherence to joint understanding and contain no surprises. The business priority is to discover and prioritize opportunities and needs while the technology priority is to offer practical solutions. The systems manager in charge of this group must represent IT to the business and must represent the business unit to IT. This position in a matrix organization requires the ability to report to multiple managers and to be an honest advocate for each. Success requires the appropriate personality, as well as the appropriate culture. Taking the time to find and train capable systems managers is critical. The organization may be right but it will not function correctly without the right people in these key positions. They need to understand the business, the personalities, and the technology without letting ego into the equation.

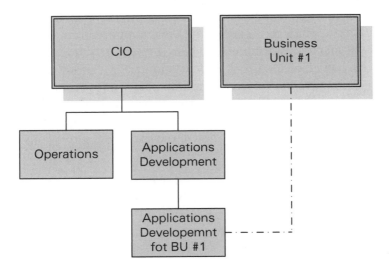

Figure 2–1 Matrix organization chart.

The systems manager is the single point of contact between business units and IT. A many-to-many relationship is counterproductive. All activity is coordinated through the systems manager, who must avoid the trap of becoming a bottleneck. A large part of this role is like that of a traffic cop, participating directly only in those activities that require a systems manager's direct involvement. The systems manager has direct control of the business unit's dedicated Applications

Development staff and coordinates the business unit's use of shared technology services.

Shared services provide specialty skills that may not have critical mass within each business unit and need to be managed for the enterprise in order to leverage skills, obtain economies of scale, and maintain an application architecture. Specialty skills may include Database Administration, Systems Administration, Help Desk service, and network administration. Shared services are traditionally almost exclusively found in infrastructure or data center groups.

Technology as a business partner has now evolved beyond this model of shared services. Personal Productivity Services are critical. They are new, shared service organizations, which do not report through the data center hierarchy.

Personal Productivity Services involve a group that integrates support personnel and personal productivity applications at the desktop and individual level. It is technology with a human face. It is comprised of the Help Desk, first- and second-level support, training, and desktop development. Desktop development was created to expose many users to the power of IT. Because of its power and direct speed of implementation and the very real and immediate improvement in quality of life, this very quick response to individual and small group needs (repeated for many small groups) became an opportunity to add value to the enterprise. In addition, it established relationships across the organization.

IT has become mission-critical and needs to be managed as a strategic asset. IT is inseparable from the business and requires complete alignment with business goals. Successful IT executives need to consider themselves, and convince others to consider them, as part of the business rather than separate themselves from the business by managing risks and expectations.

III. Thou shalt build and cultivate relationships inside and outside the enterprise.

Good relationships are critical for good partnerships. Relationships need to be continually nurtured. Relationships need to become institutionalized. Relationships need to be grown beyond individual relationships to departmental relationships. The relationship must be viewed as value-added. A partner's perspective and needs must be anticipated. A good partner answers a question before it is asked.

Relationships, while strongly encouraged on an individual level, need to be understood on a group level. For example, if a particularly difficult partner has been unable to form a relationship with technology staff, the technology department must recognize this and take steps to forge the right relationships. This should require senior technology managers to identify the sources of the relationship problem and actively correct them. This may involve issues of competence, mutual respect, credibility, business knowledge and perspective, or communications, etc. Relationships are not built overnight and require patience and consistency.

IV. Thou shalt design an infrastructure that's a competitive advantage.

For decades, IT organizations have been labeled as cost centers and IT infrastructures are one of the primary reasons for this much-deserved label. In the 1980s, most of IT's customers abandoned the centralized Infrastructure Services Organization to develop and deploy their own client-server applications. Centralized IT was too bureaucratic and costly. Today, those same customers have felt the pain of trying to support their own mini-IT operations and, quite frankly, are willing to give up their part-time technology/Infrastructure Services role. They need help, but in order to win over their business, IT still must re-engineer itself to provide a better level of service by:

- Clearly recognizing, demonstrating, and delivering value in line with the business
- Replacing or outsourcing inadequate, underperforming IT operations
- Satisfying rapid ramp-up and/or multi-location infrastructure requirements
- Gaining/maintaining market advantage with leading edge technology and services
- Reducing IT support costs and improving cost controls

A new approach is for IT to become an ITSP by:

- Aligning behaviors, processes, and technologies along value streams
- Transitioning back-office IT into a fullscale development and support environment
- Architecting and implementing complex networks and hosting environments that applications require
- Satisfying demanding new service levels
- Converting IT staff's mindset from "internal support" to that of a service provider

Keep in mind that once processes are streamlined and effective, your house (infrastructure) will support the new enterprise. Then, you will need to advertise your services. Yes, services are what matters. People need business problems solved, not technology offerings to admire. Once you transition your infrastructure to that of an ITSP and get your house in order, customers will come.

V. Thou shalt focus on the customer.

Four elements are key to providing good customer service:

- Identify your key customers
- Identify key services of key customers
- Identify key processes that support key services
- Communicate with customers often via a process

Don't just talk about improving communication, and don't just rely on monthly or quarterly get-togethers. Networked computing has destroyed whatever little communication there was between IT and its customers as well as internally within IT. A process that promotes and instills effective communication practices on a daily basis must be implemented.

The primary function of the Production Acceptance process (discussed in Chapter 5) is to promote effective communication practices for deploying, implementing, and supporting mission-critical network computing systems. It is the most critical process for improving communications between IT and the business, within IT, and especially between Applications Development and operational support.

VI. Thou shalt honor time-tested disciplines (standards, processes, etc.).

- Processes shall be streamlined
- Implementation shall be minimum yet sufficient
- Control shall be centralized

Whether your company has a mainframe environment or not, it is crucial to understand the importance of mainframe disciplines, processes, procedures, standards, and guidelines. In the age of distributed everything-to-everywhere, disciplines are more important than ever. You cannot, however, simply transplant mainframe disciplines onto network computing environments. You need to customize and streamline these disciplines so that they can manage a modern, chaotic, heterogeneous infrastructure. By necessity, the mainframe environment was large, complex, and enjoyed the luxury of timely planning. Today's client-server and Web-enabled environments need the same type of structure and discipline with more streamlining.

There are many system management processes (see Figure 2–2) to implement but please don't attempt to take them all on unless you have an unlimited resource pool. Implement the handful that are most critical to your environment. From the 200 companies (Fortune 500 and Global 2000) we've studied, very few have the most critical set of processes, and if they do, they're not very effective. In our opinion, the most critical set of processes are:

- Production Acceptance
- Change Management
- Problem Management
- Security
- Business Continuity

Because most IT shops already have implemented security procedures, the focus needs to be getting the other disciplines properly implemented.

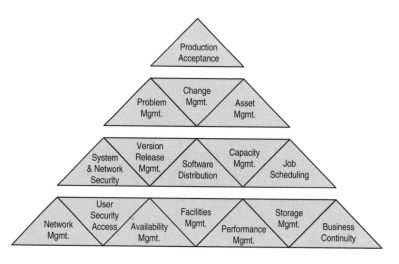

Figure 2–2 System management processes.

Develop minimum, yet sufficient, enterprise-wide standards, architectures, documentation, etc., for each area of IT, including the network, data center, desktops, development tools, nomadic computers, servers, and so on. You need standards for today, and clear statements of direction for your standards (environments, platforms, paradigms, or architectures—you pick the buzzword) in the future.

Centralized control means controlling costs by developing architectures, and deploying standards from a central location, for example:

- Global Standard Network
- Global Standard Desktop Hardware
- Global Standard Desktop Operating System
- Global Standard Desktop Application Suite
- Global Standard Virus Scanning
- Global Standard Server Hardware
- Global Standard Server Operating System
- Global Standard Data Backup
- Global Standard Messaging & Collaboration Platform
- Global Standard Monitoring
- Global Standard Remote Access
- Global Standard Development Database

- Global Standard Application Distribution Platform
- Global Standard Development Methods and Tools

Without standards and centralized control of key enterprise-wide processes, it will be futile to attempt to build a cost-effective, world-class organization.

VII. Thou shalt demonstrate and convey the value of IT throughout the enterprise.

Today, IT professionals need to walk with the great unwashed and communicate with customers. We need to schmooze, sell, and otherwise promote our services. IT organizations need to sell the fact that IT can and should be leveraged for business value and growth to their business colleagues. True commitment requires educated understanding. It is the job of the CIO to demonstrate the relationship between understanding of strategic technology initiatives and the long-term success of the firm. If executive management fails to see the value of their involvement, it is the CIO's role to change that perception or to think about his next career move.

Value should be quantifiable and measurable. It is best to communicate value in its simplest recognizable form. For an example of this concept, consider the following two paragraphs:

Unedited Version	Value Communication Version
We built a robust, flexible Editorial platform that is scalable and automates the editorial process, utilizing redirectional metadata technology to deliver abstract, encapsulated information.	We built a reliable and flexible Editorial tool that gathers, presents, and delivers customized information to our clients. The tool reduces product creation time by 40 percent and can deliver information in any industry standard format without requiring technical intervention.

Value is best communicated to the enterprise by IT's business partners. The right relationship and recognition of value leads to the ideal situation of business partners becoming evangelists. At a fundamental level, it needs to be understood (without having to say so) that the partnering relationship is the underpinning of the entire process of value creation. All members of IT need to be educated to recognize their business contributions. All need to understand their business partner's concerns and address them both formally and informally.

VIII. Thou shalt establish and uphold a common set of shared values.

Values are guiding principles—basic beliefs that are the fundamental assumptions upon which all subsequent actions are based. Quality of life leads to success. As a whole, values define the personality and character of an individual or a group. Values are the essence of an individual or group and provide guidelines by which to make consistent decisions. In reality, values are ideals that are indicative of one's vision of how the world should work.

Values form a contract between the individuals and the group, as exhibited in the following examples. If all staff members are making decisions based upon the same values, it is more likely that:

- Delegation of responsibility and authority will function effectively
- Thousands of individual decisions will converge in a consistent strategy
- Synergies will be realized
- Partnerships will prosper
- Productivity will accelerate
- Retention will never be a problem
- The firm will reap large profits

Appropriate values inexorably lead to principled actions and a high quality of life: they are a guide to hiring decisions; they establish a common culture; they foster strategic decision making (even short term, tactical decisions made by guiding principles are strategic); and they lay the groundwork for internal consistency.

IX. Thou shalt focus with the same intensity on organization, people, and process components as thou does on technology and development!

Please give non-technology initiatives equal billing!

X. Thou Shalt measure and benchmark!

If you don't know the numbers, you cannot cost-effectively manage the environment. IT professionals need to focus on two objectives. The first is improving the efficiency and effectiveness of IT—that is, getting more things done faster and better with the same or fewer resources. The second is demonstrating the value of IT to the enterprise. The key to both of these is *measurement*. In the first case, IT performance is measured so that there is a benchmark against which to improve. In the second case, measures are used that connote value, whether that value is expressed by reducing the cost of doing business or by new revenue streams that are the direct result of an investment in information technology.

Metrics by themselves provide little value—it is how the metrics are implemented, reported, and acted upon that differentiates successful measurement programs from failures.

Summary

This chapter began by listing the 24 top IT issues that confront CIOs today. We followed this up with recommendations focusing on organization, people, process, and technology. These proposed solutions form the foundation of our 10 commandments for building the ideal IT environment, which we described at the conclusion of this chapter.

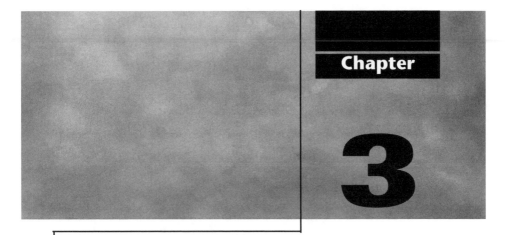

Chapter

3

IT Assessments, Planning, and Development

Introduction

This chapter begins by describing the need for and the value of conducting professional IT assessments and planning and development workshops to improve an organization's efficiency, especially in regard to its infrastructure. We explain the critical factors of *buy-in* and support and describe how to acquire them. Next, we outline how to perform a typical one day IT assessment to highlight specific problem areas, and how to conduct a multiple day planning and development workshop to brainstorm solutions to these problems. Finally, we list over 80 common infrastructure issues compiled from conducting dozens of these workshops around the world.

The Need for Assessments and Planning and Development Workshops

Since client-server (or, if you prefer, *network*) computing burst on the scene in the late 1980s, executives have had a difficult time trying to cost-effectively manage their mission-critical production environments. Executives who are chartered to design and manage world class environments are frustrated, blaming it on the technology and lack of discipline. For the past two decades, these executives have reorganized at least a dozen times and have endeavored to implement a few critical-system management processes, though to no avail. As it turns out, most of them have failed miserably. We are here to tell you why, and to show you what it takes to build an ideal IT organization. In addition, this ideal IT environment will establish a solid foundation that will facilitate stability and growth for all IT organizations, regardless of size. We recommend the following two very important programs:

- The IT Assessment
- The IT Planning and Development Workshop

These programs are designed to support small- to large-scale initiatives that require IT cooperatives to come together, plan, and support change and growth. These initiatives should be performed sequentially as part of a complete initiative. Each program provides your organization with the tools and output necessary to address the organization, people, and process issues inherent in your operation. The biggest problems in the industry are not based on technology. They arise when dealing with the organizational, people, and process issues. Later in this chapter, we describe the specific issues found within these areas.

Struggling With The Issues

In our experience, we have yet to witness a growing or struggling IT organization that is weak in technology and strong in the areas of organization and production processes. Every symptom apparent in the operation of technology-oriented installations, including:

- Unstable network environments and operations
- Unstable server environments and operations
- Problematic data feeds, loads, and integrity
- Inefficient Problem Management scheme

have all been traced back to underlining issues of poor organizational structure and the lack of robust processes. The same is also true in early stages or start-up situations, posing different symptoms and threats that include:

- Poor planning for future operations
- Inability to keep up with growth demands

For example, some of the underlining issues involve:

Ineffective Organizational Structures

Most of the issues in IT are caused by organizational structure. Organizations are ineffective. Their focus is on technology vs. focusing on mission-critical production systems. Most of them are also missing the key function (PS) to ensure high availability and improve customer service. For the rest of the issues, see Table 3–3 and Table 3–7.

Neglected People Issues

Creating the proper career path for junior staff is being put on the back burner. One of the key reasons that made the mainframe era so successful was not the technology—it was breeding junior staff directly from the data center. Staff members were reared with RAS. For a list of all the people issues, see Table 3–7.

Missing or Ineffective Processes

Critical system management processes are rarely effective primarily due to two reasons—lack of a PS function (centralized ownership and accountability of key processes) or *buy-in* and *commitment* throughout the organization. For a list of many of the process issues, Table 3–5 and Table 3–7.

Neglected Management Responsibilities

Management is just as busy as anyone else. Many critical management responsibilities are neglected (i.e., leadership, direction, etc.). While just about everyone is trying to do more with fewer resources, management responsibilities need to remain constant in order to build an effective team. For a list of many of the management issues see Table 3–4 and Table 3–7.

Lack of Effective Communication Practices

With the number of issues highlighted throughout this book, how can any organization have effective communication practices? They don't exist. For a list of many of the process issues, see Table 3–6 and Table 3–7.

We reiterate that in addressing these issues we hope to change not only the mindset of the CIO but ultimately obtain *buy-in* and *commitment* from the entire organization. Our objective is not to advertise or sell IT assessments and workshops, but rather to sell you on what it will take to build the ideal IT organization. This is the difference—this is what we are bringing to the table.

Selling the CIO

We now understand why IT executives in this economy cringe at the thought of spending another dime on another IT assessment or executive planning workshop. They're tired of assessing and planning. They would very much like to start successfully implementing a few much-needed processes and addressing some of the people issues. If we were in their shoes, we would feel the same way. After all, most CIOs have been involved with many IT assessments and workshops usually facilitated by very large consulting firms with very hefty price tags. The deliverables typically have plenty of good content. The key word is *plenty*. Many times it is too much to digest and too much to implement. An acknowledgement of the deliverable and enthusiasm for executing the recommendations becomes evident, when CIOs hold their weekly staff meetings where they discuss and prioritize their goals based on the plan. Soon thereafter, very little is actually implemented due to the pending projects and constant emergencies (fire-fighting). After three or four staff meetings, the deliverable usually ends up sitting around on an executive's shelving collecting dust. This is why executives cringe at the mere thought of another assessment or workshop.

Contrary to the above, what we are recommending is different—minimal, yet sufficient content. Our recommended method of evaluating and providing recommendations is more effective than the typical assessments and workshops because we primarily concentrate on the most critical organization, people, and process issues. Most consultants tend to focus on many issues, most of which are technology-related. This explains why companies spend so much money on the latest and greatest gadgets and expect the staff to support them, while the organization, technically speaking, falls apart. This is one of the reasons why it is important to make a unified decision involving all of the components of an organization.

The Key to Successfully Building the Ideal IT Organization

The key can be summed up in one word—*buy-in*! To properly address the organization, people, and process issues, and make IT organizations successful, *buy-in* from every department of the organization is an essential element. Dealing with people issues is not rocket science and implementing processes is not complicated either. Many processes are already documented in books (i.e., *IT Systems Management* by Rich Schiesser). Effectively utilizing these processes is another ball game (actually another sport altogether). The difficulty lies in getting *buy-in* across the board starting with your technical staff, next your Help Desk staff, then management, etc. So, if we're trying to sell you anything, it is the importance of *buy-in*.

How to Acquire *Buy-in*

There is only one way to acquire *buy-in* from all key staff members within the organization and that is to get all the players (especially the less-than-candid politician types—every organization has them) in the same room to highlight all the issues, brainstorm recommendations, and develop a plan to implement those recommendations. There is no other method of addressing these types of issues than holding a workshop. Whatever solutions arise to address the organizational, people, and process issues must obtain *buy-in* from everyone or the endeavor to build the ideal IT environment will be futile. This entire process or exercise will fall into the same category as other workshops—a temporary and short-lived team building exercise.

What makes this workshop like no other is our primary objective. Our objective is to get *buy-in* from the bottom-up first. Getting *buy-in* from the CIO is not enough. In order to successfully move forward and implement the recommendations that come out of the workshop, *buy-in* MUST come from all levels of the organization (technical, non-technical, and management). *Buy-in* is a firm *commitment* by the organization to execute one plan. This is why an extensive assessment and an intensive workshop are essential to laying out the foundation and establishing *commitment*, approval, and support throughout the organization to build this elusive, world class IT environment. It is doable!

Not Another Assessment

So, you ask...Why another assessment? Why not just a workshop? Well, although most executives have a pretty good idea of what the issues are, the primary reason for requiring an IT assessment is to make sure your workshop facilitators and executive management understand and agree on all the issues prior to the workshop. Based on previous assessments, we can pretty much guarantee that executive managers already know what their issues are. The assessment is primarily geared for your workshop facilitators. It is critical that the facilitators understand and feel the same type of pain as the organization. When you go in search of the ideal IT environment, you will find that an external consultant can be of great assistance to your organization as an unbiased IT professional assessor.

The Facilitator

External consultants should conduct a one to three day assessment of your IT department, depending on the size of the organization. These assessments must take a high level panoramic view of IT initiatives and issues within the infrastructure. Consultants must meet with key personnel, management, and technicians. The process should involve 30-minute interviews with middle level IT managers, senior executives, and key technical staff. We say this because technicians in most companies have a better and—more importantly—an unbiased understanding than management of the infrastructure and related issues. Just as critical, most technicians do not have hidden agendas. Managers often come to the table with excess baggage, including territorial and political conflicts.

The interviews should be conducted to assess the key issues in the areas of organization, people, and process. Once these interviews have been held, you should meet with your sponsor to share notes, validate information, and obtain input to complete the analysis. At this point, it should be determined whether it is necessary to interview additional key personnel to acquire additional data.

Analyze the outputs of the assessment and develop an outline of written initial recommendations to support the initiative. Then, meet with the customer once again to present the recommendations and gain final feedback. Once the assessment has been completed, the analysis and initial recommendations are to be submitted to the CIO in a *minimal, yet sufficient* written report evaluating the IT organization. In addition, prepare preliminary input material for the IT planning and development workshop. To simplify matters, we have included some key notes that, if adhered to, can streamline the process.

Keep It Simple

A one to three day (maximum) assessment of an organization is challenging. Even more challenging, however, is assembling the results of these reports—which are, to say the least, disappointing. Adhering to the following guidelines facilitates the process of assessing an organization:

- Keep things simple—*minimum yet sufficient* content
- Provide no more than five recommendations that would have a significant impact on resolving the most critical issues
- Provide a list of key methodologies (The Ten Commandments— See Chapter 2); these methodologies become part of the overall vision when designing and implementing the ideal IT organization
- Allot 35 to 45 minutes for interviewing 15 to 20 staff and management personnel

- Allot an additional 30 minutes to interview (at the very least) two customers of IT services
- Every aspect of the IT organization has to be continuously scrutinized to see if it is a candidate for reengineering
- Sort the issues into five categories: *Organization, People, Process, IT Management, and Communication*

Key Pointers

The following are some additional points to keep in mind when performing an assessment:

Organization

- Understand current industry problems (see Table 3–3 and Table 3–7)
- Assess the ineffectiveness of the current organizational structure
- Determine what it will take to transition an ineffective organization into an effective organization
- Evaluate how these changes can be effectively implemented without too much disruption
- Determine the key players

People

- Understand current industry problems (see Table 3–7)
- Gather data regarding the issues
- Evaluate the situation and how it effects the entire organization
- Evaluate how management can better manage its most critical resources and its issues

Processes

- Understand current industry problems (see Table 3–5 and Table 3–7)
- Assess the organization and determine which processes are missing and which are ineffective

- Determine the key players and what it will take to acquire their *buy-in*
- Identify the major obstacles (i.e., organizational, people, and processes, etc.)

IT Management

- Understand current industry problems (see Table 3–4 and Table 3–7).
- Determine which processes (if any) could potentially improve the situation

Communication

- Understand current industry problems (see Table 3–6 and Table 3–7).
- Evaluate current organization structure for barriers or silos between departments
- Evaluate current processes for effectiveness
- Determine which organizational and process changes could potentially improve the situation

We advise the customer to allot time for all members within the organization who are affected by troubling issues (and thus by change) to participate in the assessments and workshops.

The Role of Organization

To make the assessment a success, the organization should set aside a specific time for all those participating in the interviews, and format those interviews as follows:

Facilitator's requirements from the customer

- Ability to have a 30 to 45 minute meeting with executive management to establish a relationship and acquire initial program *buy-in*
- Ability to meet (30 minutes) separately with middle level management from Operations, Applications Development,

Architecture, Help Desk, Networking, Database Administration, etc.

- Ability to meet (30 minutes) separately with one or two technical people from Systems Administration, one DBA, one Help Desk person, one Desktop Services person, and anyone else that might provide good insight into the issues
- Would like to meet with at least two IT customers (30 minutes each)

Once all interviews have been conducted, the deliverable from the assessment should include a report outlining:

- High-level understanding of the business environment—business units supported, key business objectives and drivers, customers, markets and trends, and the regulatory environment
- High-level understanding of the IT service delivery environment—IT services required to support the business, service objectives, and SLA agreements (formal and informal); includes services provided directly to business units and other areas of the IT organization
- High-level understanding of the overall IT environment: policies, technology architectures, facilities, processes, and organization
- Key issues and challenges from all levels of the organization
- Prioritized list of the minimum and sufficient set of recommendations (no more than 3–5)

Once all of the data has been gathered, all inquiries have been made, and the information has been evaluated, ask yourself:

- How can I correct these imperfections that, in essence, have been creating so many problems for this organization?
- How can I successfully build the ideal IT organization?
- How can I transform this organization into an ideal IT organization?

The answer lies in changing the pronoun from *I* to *we*. One has to realize that it takes the effort and impetus of an entire organization to turn an ineffective (mediocre) organization into a world-class organization.

These assessments (interviews) are important because everyone needs to understand what is ailing the organization, diagnose the problem, and consequently prescribe a remedy. We recommend making the discussions positive, lively, and interactive—discussions that will lead the organization up the path towards excellence. Consequently, it is the best way to assure and ensure *buy-in* from everyone from every level throughout the organization. It is the only way to ensure a successful re-engineering of an organization and its future projects.

Summary of the Assessment Process

Begin with Analyzing the Current Organizational Structure.

If at all possible, try to obtain a copy of the organization's structure from your sponsor before starting the assessment. It is important to analyze the structure (i.e., learn the various functions, roles and responsibilities, problem areas, and so on) before meeting with executive management so you ask the right questions.

Understand the Company's Business, Vision, and Strategy.

Is there an enterprise vision? Always keep in mind that IT's objective is to successfully partner with the business. IT needs to be organized to rapidly respond to the needs of individual business groups. This requires a planning process tightly integrated with each of the business groups and an enterprise-wide vision within which all of these needs can be met. IT has become mission critical and needs to be managed as a strategic asset. It is inseparable from the business and requires complete alignment with business goals. Successful IT executives need to consider themselves (and convince others to consider them) part of the business rather than separate from the business.

This is important because it is not just about *buy-in* to one plan and execution thereof—it is about walking together as a coalesced organization with a vision and a strategy. The impetus of *all as one* will make the organization stronger and the efforts and achievements that much sweeter when they see their objectives have been met.

Understand IT's Vision and Major Initiatives.

Does IT have a strategic vision that's aligned with the enterprise vision? To align with the business, IT needs to be able to react both functionally (e.g., expert technical skills) and geographically (e.g., globally, regionally, locally) to business imperatives with flexibility.

Identify Key Personnel in the Organization.

Ask your executive sponsor who the key players are. Who are the organization's most valuable resources/contributors? It's critical that these individuals are interviewed.

Conduct 30 minute interviews to assess the key issues in the areas of organization, people, and process.

Keep the discussions short and to the point. Start out by telling the interviewer that their discussion is about organization, people, and process issues only—*not technology*. Start the interview process by only asking one question: "What works and what doesn't?" Or, rephrase it and say: "You commute to work each day—are there any barriers or obstacles that inhibit you from being a productive contributor?"

Once the interviews have been conducted, assess the data and meet with executive management (sponsor) to share notes, validate data, and obtain additional input to complete the analysis (if required).

After the one to three day assessment is complete, you should have a pretty good idea of what the issues and recommendations are—make sure you meet with your executive sponsor to debrief him/her before completing the engagement.

Analyze data and develop a report with recommendations (keep it under fifty pages).

It should take you one to two weeks to finalize the report. Make sure you keep the recommendations minimum and sufficient—no more than three to five recommendations.

Present the findings to the CIO.

Meet with the CIO and his/her direct reports (if possible) to present the findings.

IT Planning and Development Workshop

If preceded by the assessment, once the fact-finding and preliminary recommendations have been completed, an outside team (third party) will need to facilitate a three-day offsite session with key members of the customer's organization.

The workshop is not one of those typical offsite management planning sessions. This program is designed to bring key contributors (technical and management) from all areas of the organization into one room to brainstorm the issues, prioritize the issues, and develop a *playbook*. This is an action plan with associated milestones and responsibilities clearly noted with due dates that everyone, including the CIO, has bought into—*one plan* into which the entire organization has bought! Remember that when we say *buy-in*, we mean *commitment* to execute on the plan on behalf of the entire organization. Full support and approval from the CIO needs to be communicated to technical staff if massive improvements are to take place.

On Common Ground

What makes this workshop like no other? It's the process we undertake to acquire *buy-in* and *commitment*. The key to a successful workshop and, more importantly, post workshop follow through, is moving forward as a cohesive unit. Management and staff as one create a plan (playbook) to build that elusive ideal organization.

Our proven method in moving forward with *one* plan is making sure that all participants in the workshop are equal in status—in other words, all ranks (technical leads, project managers, managers, and so on) are left outside the door of the workshop. Nobody is allowed to pull rank during the workshop. This is exactly what we do and in most cases (9 out of 10) the staff's recommendations are used versus management's in the final decision making process. Management's view of the environment is usually tainted with political agendas or personal aspirations and the technical staff have no hidden agendas.

Unfortunately, but typically true when executive management decides to restructure the organization, they do so with very little staff consultation. Consequently, they decide one day to surprise the staff with their new organizational structure—never taking into account the advice or opinion of the staff. These are the individuals in the trenches that actually confront the issues, we discuss throughout the book, on a daily basis. As usual, most of the staff don't react well to these types of changes.

What's wrong with including key individuals throughout the organization in the decision making process? Not a thing, if you value your resources to use their wisdom. Generally speaking the staff tends to know more regarding what's going on or perhaps not going on in your IT environment than any executive could ever see perched in their ivory tower. Management has their view of how the organization should be structured, but the people who have the *best* view are the ones in the trenches. After all, they see the obstacles and problems on a daily basis. Why wouldn't you find it wise to include their input in the decision making process?

Workshop Objectives

The workshop is intended to facilitate the identification of specific issues and the development of an intelligent, practical plan of action that has the *buy-in*, *commitment*, and *ownership* of key representatives within the entire IT organization. Once the action plan is in place, specific remediation projects can be conducted with an appropriate level of confidence that they are the right things to be working on, that they are occurring in the right sequence, and that they are given the appropriate priority for completion.

The primary objectives of the workshop are to:

- Highlight, categorize, and prioritize the top 3–5 IT-related issues
- Develop an action plan to address the top issues
- Design the appropriate organizational structure
- Get *buy-in* and *commitment* from all IT (staff, management, and executive management)
- Improve communication between the groups (team building)

These objectives can be achieved if you have experienced facilitators and participants who are frustrated with their current environment and are ready for change.

Workshop Schedule

The presentation is in the approach, therefore the deliverable has to address all of the issues (see Figure 3–1). The playbook outlines the plan to be executed. This plan is similar to the organization's deliverance from its current, daily hell to an opportunity for some heavenly changes.

DAY 1—Participants should include key management staff, but not the CXO. The objectives of this first session will be to:

- Provide synopsis and objectives of the workshop
- Identify business issues and initiatives
- Highlight industry related IT organization, people, and process issues
- Acquire thorough understanding of the current organization structure, its history, and its evolution
- Discuss and brainstorm IT issues
- Develop a plan to address the prioritized issues
- Work with the team to construct the proper organization structure (based on 200 assessments and dozens of workshops, it's the number one issue) and a plan to address the top three to five issues

---

DAY 2—Off-site session will be held with key members of the technical staff. The objectives of this session will be to:

- Provide synopsis and objectivs of the workshop
- Gain a general understanding of the enviroment and its issues
- Highlight industry related IT organization, people, and process issues
- Acquire thorough understanding of current organization structure, its history, and its evolution
- Discuss and brainstorm IT issues
- Organize, categorize, and prioritize the (brainstormed) issues
- Develop a plan to address the prioritized issues
- Work with the team to construct the proper organization structure and a plan to address the top three to five issues
- Prepare presentation for Day 1 management team
- Present findings to management team

DAY 3—Particpants will include the management team and key staff members. The objectives of this session are:

- Compare and debate findings from Day 1 and Day 2 attendees
- Develop one plan (playbook) with a new organization structure and the top three to five issues to address
- Prepare presentation to CXO
- Present to CXO
- Acquire *buy-in* and *commitment* to move forward with the playbook

Figure 3–1 Schedule for workshop.

Workshop Deliverables

Workshop deliverables should include:

- Structured, facilitated workshop
- Preliminary migration approach
- Key organizational issues, opportunities for improvement, and recommended solutions
- An action plan developed by the workshop participants
- Across the board *buy-in* of the action plan

Post Workshop

It is as important to us as it is to the organization that the participants being assessed (in this case, the managers and technicians) come away with a clearer understanding of:

- The top organizational, people, and process issues in IT
- How to build the ideal IT organization
- How to properly structure the organization and which functions are critical for success
- The minimum and sufficient processes, removing the bureaucracy, and implementing a cost-effective infrastructure
- The key methodologies for designing, implementing, and supporting a global IT organization
- The obstacles
- How to manage technology as a strategic asset rather than managing technology as a cost center
- The importance of aligning and partnering with the business and becoming part of the business rather than being apart from the business
- How to do more with less
- How to address the top people issues
- The importance of recognizing and communicating value to the enterprise

Wrap-Up

Candidly speaking, the reason why we are dealing with so many organizational, people, and process issues today is quite simple. For many years now, executive management's primary focus has continued to be investing their finances in new technology and pushing their people forward to produce performance-ready products at record speed. Here is an analogy:

> Although the blood is still circulating throughout the body (the organization), the skeletal make-up is progressively deteriorating. Members of the body (organization) such as the lower level personnel as well as the executive managers start to experience pain and eventually there is internal bleeding. It is not until then that they realize something is definitely wrong and that an immediate diagnosis (assessment) of the situation, accompanied by an immediate cure (resolution) is in demand.

So what we are trying to say is that performing an assessment of the entire IT organization, followed by a high level workshop, will bring all the pieces together, even if it means restructuring the organization. This is essential to the creation of a world class organization. Nevertheless, the absolute support and approval (*buy-in*) of executive management and its entire organization is key to the success thereof.

The Issues

Over the past several years, we have conducted numerous IT planning and development workshops at dozens of major companies worldwide. At these workshops, to identify issues that were impeding the success of their organizations and to brainstorm methods for addressing these deficiencies, we met with key personnel—including team leaders, supervisors, and managers. After analyzing thousands of issues, we determined that 82 of them were frequently reoccurring and could be grouped into five categories of resolution. The entire list is shown in Appendix C. The resolution categories are organization, people, process, IT management, and communication. Most of the issues fell into multiple resolution categories, although four of the five resolution categories each had several issues related solely to them. Table 3–1 shows the number of issues associated with each individual category, and with multiple categories.

Several aspects of Table 3–1 are noteworthy. First, it shows that the overwhelming majority of issues (51 out of 82) are properly addressed by employing more than one resolution category. This intuitively follows from the complex nature of IT, particularly infrastructure related problems. Second, most of the issues that pertain to a single resolution category fall into either the organization or process categories. This is also in line with our own experiences that most single category issues can be addressed with proper reorganization or with robust processes. Finally, the table shows there are no issues that can be resolved with people changes alone. In other words, while there are many issues involving people, their resolution usually involves a combination of approaches in the organization, process, and communication areas.

Because there are so many issues that span multiple resolution categories, it is worth examining the distribution of all problems as they pertain to each of the five groupings. Table 3–2 lists the total number of sole and combined issues associated with each category. As expected, the resolution categories having the largest number of issues associated with them are organization and process. This bolsters our position that proper organizational structure and robust processes can solve the majority of problems in today's complex infrastructures.

We will now look in more detail at each of the four resolution categories listed in Table 3–1 that have issues pertaining solely to them. Again, these categories are *organization, process, IT management*, and *communication*. Table 3–3 through Table 3–6 will list the issues associated with each of these four resolution categories. In addition, the tables will designate to what degree of likelihood a PS function would help to solve the issue.

Table 3–3 lists the issues solely relating to the *organization* resolution category. We designate each entry with a unique Issue Reference Number (Issue Ref. #). The first two digits of this three-digit number refer to the table in which it resides. The third digit is simply the entry sequence number in the table. We do this to be able to distinguish all 82 issues in the various tables without duplicating them or repeating reference numbers. These numbers are also used in the table of all issues, in Appendix C.

Table 3-1 Issues Associated with Individual and Multiple Categories

Resolution Category	Number of Issues
Solely Organization	13
Solely People	0
Solely Process	11
Solely IT Management	4
Solely Communication	3
Across Multiple Categories	51
Total	82

Table 3-2 Total Numbers of Sole and Combined Issues by Category

Resolution Category	Number of Issues from Sole and Combined Categories
Organization	54
People	24
Process	52
IT Management	17
Communication	21

In reading down the list, it is apparent that these kinds of issues involve various departments within an infrastructure, cut across multiple platforms and stem, in part, from a lack of centralization. Table 3–3 also shows that for seven of these thirteen issues there is a medium or high likelihood that these issues may be addressed with a PS function. Later in this chapter we will revisit the topic of which issues may have a high likelihood of being addressed by introducing a PS department.

In Table 3–5, we list those issues identified at the planning and development workshops pertaining solely to the *process* resolution category. Almost half of the eleven issues described in this table are directly related to the lack of a specific IT process. The first two entries focus on the lack of a marketing and Production Acceptance process. These have a high likelihood of being resolved with a PS function due to the added visibility and the more disciplined deployment structure that would result. The next two issues involve storage management and metrics and have a medium likelihood of having PS resolve them. The remaining issues cover a variety of topics and all have a low likelihood of being resolved with a PS function.

Table 3-3 Issues Identified at Planning Development Workshops Pertaining Solely to *Organization*

Issue Ref. #	Description of Issues Pertaining to *Organization*	Likelihood of Solving with PS Function
3.3.1	Three levels of Technical Support (Systems Administration) not defined	High
3.3.2	Difficult for staff to learn new technologies—preoccupied with daily "fire-fighting drills"	High
3.3.3	Tactical, not strategic, approach	High
3.3.4	IT shops are organizing based on particular technologies, i.e., Mainframe, AS/400, NT, UNIX, etc.	Medium
3.3.5	Irrational organization structure—responsibility without accountability	Medium
3.3.6	Two separate infrastructure organizations causing combative (power struggle), ineffective, inefficient, intergroup chasm between infrastructure development and production support	Medium
3.3.7	Duplicate Systems Administration functions	Low
3.3.8	Database Administration is not centralized; in many companies it's organized under Applications Development, for others in Operations Support, and yet for others it's split between the two	Low
3.3.9	Business liaison model should not be eliminated from customer perspective	Low
3.3.10	High complexity in the organizational structure	Low
3.3.11	International technical resources do not report into centralized IT	Low
3.3.12	Re-inventing the wheel—wasted resources	Low
3.3.13	LAN support is split between organizations	Low

Table 3–4 shows the four issues that relate solely to the *management* resolution category. These items involve budget matters, decision making, project priorities, and resources—items that are certainly management-oriented, but not likely to be resolved with a PS function.

Table 3–6 lists the three issues identified at our workshops that pertain solely to the *communication* resolution category. The first issue involves managing customer expectations. A PS function could help in managing customer expectations about production schedules, batch windows, and report delivery, and is shown as having a medium likelihood of resolving this issue. The other two issues involving standards and decision making for communications have a low likelihood of resolution with PS.

Table 3–4 Issues Identified at Planning Development Workshops Pertaining Solely to *Management*

Issue Ref. #	Description of Issues Pertaining to *Management*	Likelihood of Solving with PS Function
3.4.1	Increased costs for maintenance and upgrades for software to keep software in synch with changing business and technology	Low
3.4.2	Technical staff input not used in key decision making throughout IT	Low
3.4.3	IT focused on high visibility projects vs. planning—thus a separate structure focuses on production support	Low
3.4.4	Lack of management resources	Low

Table 3–5 Issues Identified at Planning Development Workshops Pertaining Solely to *Process*

Issue Ref. #	Description of Issues Pertaining to *Process*	Likelihood of Solving with PS Function
3.5.1	Lack of a process to market and sell IT services	High
3.5.2	Lack of Production Acceptance to effectively deploy network computing systems from development to production	High
3.5.3	Lack of a Storage Management process	Medium
3.5.4	Lack of defined metrics for measuring effectiveness	Medium
3.5.5	Need a balance between standards and flexibility	Low
3.5.6	Lack of a process to gauge customer productivity	Low
3.5.7	Lack of definition of what is mission critical and levels of importance to the business—prioritize	Low
3.5.8	Lack of software version control and a code migration process	Low
3.5.9	Lack of an Asset Management process	Low
3.5.10	Lack of a Capacity Planning process	Low
3.5.11	Lack of Configuration Management, both hardware and software configurations	Low

The remaining 51 issues cut across multiple resolution categories. We list these in Table 3–7. Each of the five resolution categories of *organization, people, process, IT management,* and *communication* are designated as O, E, P, M, and C in the table, as shown on its legend.

Table 3–6   Issues Identified at Planning Development Workshops Pertaining Solely to *Communication*

Issue Ref. #	Description of Issues Pertaining to *Communication*	Likelihood of Solving with PS Function
3.6.1	Increased costs for maintenance and upgrades to software to keep software in synch with changing business and technology	Medium
3.6.2	IT management and technical leads are not effectively managing customer expectations	Low
3.6.3	Lack of communication about decision making at the Director level	Low

Table 3–7   Issues Identified at Planning Development Workshops Pertaining to *Multiple Categories*

Issue Ref. #	Description of Issues Pertaining to *Multiple Categories*	O	E	P	M	C	Likelihood of Solving with PS Function
3.7.1	Lack of RAS in production environment	X	X	X			High
3.7.2	Lack of coordination between end-users and support groups			X		X	High
3.7.3	Unclear centralized ownership along with scattered responsiblities of technology and process, i.e., Change Management, Production Acceptance, and Problem Management	X		X			High
3.7.4	No internal QA Process for IT	X		X			High
3.7.5	Too many technologies deployed that cannot be effectively supported	X	X	X			High
3.7.6	Informal Level II support function	X		X			High
3.7.7	Lack of senior resources to properly mentor lower-level Technical Support staff	X		X			High
3.7.8	Inability to pool technical resources for specific projects	X	X				High
3.7.9	Lack of a Production Control function (Production QA, second-level Systems Admin, process ownership, production gatekeeper, etc.)	X	X	X			High
3.7.10	Lack of an effective enterprise-wide Change Mgmt/ Control process	X	X	X			High
3.7.11	Lack of coordinated responses to problems with appropriate escalation or inability to respond			X		X	Medium
3.7.12	Lack of a strategic plan to market/sell IT services	X		X		X	Medium

Table 3–7   Issues Identified at Planning Development Workshops Pertaining to *Multiple Categories* (Continued)

Issue Ref. #	Description of Issues Pertaining to *Multiple Categories*	Resolution Category					Likelihood of Solving with PS Function
		O	E	P	M	C	
3.7.13	Lack of service levels between operational support and Applications Development and between IT and customers	X		X			Medium
3.7.14	Recruiting/retaining/training/mentoring technical resources is difficult	X	X				Medium
3.7.15	Not enough staff to cover all support requirements	X	X				Medium
3.7.16	Lack of enterprise-wide System Management and monitoring tools or they are not fully implemented	X	X	X	X		Medium
3.7.17	Enterprise-wide Change Control notification process ineffective	X				X	Medium
3.7.18	Lack of clearly defined roles and responsibilities throughout enterprise	X		X	X		Medium
3.7.19	Poor communication within organization on all levels/barriers, walls between groups	X		X	X	X	Medium
3.7.20	Help Desk can not support all technologies for which they are responsible	X	X				Low
3.7.21	Lack of Hardware Management process	X		X	X		Low
3.7.22	Lack of respect for IT from customer base	X		X		X	Low
3.7.23	Meetings—inefficient, too many, difficult to coordinate, often changed, lack of respect for attendance, punctuality, preparation				X	X	Low
3.7.24	Customers driving technology decisions more than they should	X		X		X	Low
3.7.25	IT not seen as a strategic business partner	X				X	Low
3.7.26	Customers circumvent call process (call who they know, or who will give them answer they want)			X		X	Low
3.7.27	Business liaison interface with infrastructure (IT) support needs to be more integrated—they promise customers more than IT can deliver		X	X	X	X	Low
3.7.28	Ineffective Problem Management or lack thereof	X		X			Low
3.7.29	Lack of Testing or preproduction environment	X		X	X		Low
3.7.30	Need to do a better job of getting the technical resources aligned with the business drivers and requirements			X	X	X	Low

Issue Ref. #	Description of Issues Pertaining to *Multiple Categories*	Resolution Category					Likelihood of Solving with PS Function
		O	E	P	M	C	
3.7.31	Lack of mission and goals of IT as a whole, and the communication of goals and mission				X	X	Low
3.7.32	Multiple Help Desks—lack of integration processes and standards	X		X	X		Low
3.7.33	Split network support functions	X		X			Low
3.7.34	Ineffective Project Management and resources	X	X	X		X	Low
3.7.35	Lack of a Tape Librarian function	X	X	X			Low
3.7.36	Lack of a process to benchmark services	X	X	X			Low
3.7.37	Lack of centralized, empowered Project Management methodology/process	X		X			Low
3.7.38	Help Desk provides inadequate and/or incorrect information for problem resolution	X		X	X		Low
3.7.39	Unclear decision making process, inputs, parameters			X		X	Low
3.7.40	Philosophy is to say "yes" to customer regardless of their demands; customer perception is the inverse—more common	X			X		Low
3.7.41	Overreliance on consultants	X	X				Low
3.7.42	Need "all-IT" meetings on a regular basis				X	X	Low
3.7.43	Lack of a security policy and staff to manage security	X		X	X		Low
3.7.44	The centralized IT group is perceived to be in a glass house/ivory tower environment			X		X	Low
3.7.45	Lack of standards and adherence to standards throughout the infrastructure—the enterprise	X		X	X		Low
3.7.46	Lack of an effective Architecture/Planning function to design the proper infrastructure	X		X			Low
3.7.47	Lack of proper curriculum to transition and mentor staff; the consequence is a lack of technical career development program	X	X	X	X		Low
3.7.48	Ineffective global coordination	X		X	X	X	Low
3.7.49	Lack of internal and external Service Level Agreements	X		X			Low
3.7.50	Lack of a Disaster Recovery process	X	X	X	X		Low
3.7.51	Multiple support groups, roles, and responsibilities unclear for customers, i.e., desktop hardware group, desktop software group, and desktop project group	X				X	Low

The advantage of this setup is that it visually shows which issues are spread across most categories, and also which categories contain the most issues. We will not go through each issue individually, but we will reference those whose likelihood of being resolved with a PS function is high or medium. Table 3–8 lists all of these issues, regardless of what individual or multiple resolution categories they pertain. As the table shows, an overwhelming number of these issues pertain to the organization category, with the process category as a close second. Only one issue involves communication, and none of the issues relate to the management category. This tells us that, when designing and implementing a PS function, a fair number of organization and process issues may be addressed, but not those of management and communication. We list all issues in Table 3–9, regardless of individual or multiple resolution categories, that have a medium likelihood of being resolved with a PS function. The table shows how the first four entries pertain only to the organization category, but the remaining ones are fairly evenly spread across all categories. This indicates that while the likelihood of resolution is slightly lower than the issues listed in Table 3–8, the likelihood of it touching most of the categories is much higher. This means that these issues may have more widespread effect when addressed.

Table 3-8 Production Services HIGH Resolution Issues

Issue Ref. #	Description of Issues Pertaining to *Multiple Categories*	Resolution Category					Likelihood of Solving with PS Function
		O	E	P	M	C	
3.3.1	Three levels of Technical Support (Systems Administration) not defined	X					High
3.3.2	Difficult for staff to learn new technologies preoccupied with daily "fire-fighting drills"	X					High
3.3.3	Tactical, not strategic, approach	X					High
3.4.1	Lack of a process to market and sell IT services			X			High
3.4.2	Lack of a Production Acceptance process to effectively transition mission critical production applications from development to Operations			X			High
3.7.1	Lack of RAS in production environment	X	X	X			High
3.7.2	Lack of coordination between end-users and support groups			X		X	High

Table 3–8 Production Services HIGH Resolution Issues (Continued)

Issue Ref. #	Description of Issues Pertaining to *Multiple Categories*	Resolution Category					Likelihood of Solving with PS Function
		O	E	P	M	C	
3.7.3	Unclear centralized ownership along with scattered responsibilities of technology and processes, i.e., Change Mgmt, Production Acceptance, Problem Mgmt	X		X			High
3.7.4	Lack of an effective QA process for IT	X		X			High
3.7.5	Too many technologies deployed that cannot be effectively supported	X	X	X			High
3.7.6	Informal Level 2 Support function	X		X			High
3.7.7	Lack of senior resources to mentor lower level Technical Support staff	X		X			High
3.7.8	Inability to pool technical resources for specific projects	X	X				High
3.7.9	Lack of a Production Control function (Production QA, second-level Systems Admin, process ownership, gatekeepers, etc.)	X	X	X			High
3.7.10	Lack of an effective enterprise-wide Change Management/Control process	X	X	X			High

Summary

This chapter began with a discussion on the need and the value of conducting professional IT assessments and workshops. We described how these sessions could improve an IT organization's efficiency, especially in regard to the infrastructure. We next explained how critical the factors of *buy-in* and support really are to the success of these efforts, and how to go about acquiring them. Then we outlined how to perform both a one-day IT assessment to highlight specific problem areas, as well as a multiple-day planning and development workshop to brainstorm solutions to these problems. Finally, we listed over 80 common infrastructure issues compiled from conducting dozens of these workshops around the world, and organized these in issues by category. These issues show both the commonality of infrastructure problems and the fact that the majority of them are solved with organizational solutions.

Table 3–9 Production Services MEDIUM Resolution Issues

Issue Ref. #	Description of Issues	Resolution Category					Likelihood of Solving with PS Function
		O	E	P	M	C	
3.3.4	IT shops are organizing based on particular technologies, i.e, Mainframe, AS/400, NT, UNIX, etc.	X					Medium
3.3.5	Irrational organization structure—responsibility without accountability	X					Medium
3.3.6	Two separate Infrastructure Organizations causing combative (power struggle), ineffective, inefficient, inter-group chasm between infrastructure Development and Production Support	X					Medium
3.3.7	Duplicate Systems Administration functions	X					Medium
3.4.3	Lack of a Storage Management process			X			Medium
3.4.4	Lack of defined metrics for measuring the effectiveness of IT			X			Medium
3.6.1	IT Management and Technical leads are not effectively managing customer expectations					X	Medium
3.7.11	Lack of coordinated responses to problems with appropriate escalation or inability to respond			X		X	Medium
3.7.12	Lack of strategic plan to market/sell IT services	X		X			Medium
3.7.13	Lack of service levels between Operational Support and Applications Development and between IT and customers	X		X			Medium
3.7.14	Recruiting/training/mentoring technical resources is difficult	X	X				Medium
3.7.15	Not enough staff to cover all support requirements	X		X			Medium
3.7.16	Lack of enterprise-wide system management and monitoring tools or thay are not fully implemented	X	X	X	X		Medium
3.7.17	Enterprise-wide Change Control notification process ineffective	X				X	Medium
3.7.18	Lack of clear roles and responsibilities throughout enterprise	X		X	X		Medium
3.7.19	Poor communication within organization on all levels/ barriers, walls between groups	X		X	X	X	Medium

Production Services (PS)

Introduction

This chapter begins with a description of the primary responsibilities of a Production Services (PS) function within an IT infrastructure. We then show that chief among its responsibilities is to serve as a communication liaison among the various key departments within IT, and to key customer departments outside of IT. In this discussion of customer communication, we include the key element of negotiating mutually agreed-upon Service Level Agreements (SLAs). Next, we discuss the critical importance of a three tier support structure, and itemize many of the roles and responsibilities associated with each level of support. Finally, we will conclude with a summary of major infrastructure problems solved with a PS department.

Roles and Responsibilities

PS consists of Production Acceptance (prior to and during deployment of new systems), a production support function for the ongoing running of production systems, maintenance, and *fix when broken*. PS is the QA function for infrastructure development and support. Its primary role is to ensure that the production environment does not get contaminated by systems that are not thoroughly tested by going through a software development QA process and documenting the systems thoroughly. PS also ensures that these same systems have also gone through a Production Acceptance process.

The primary responsibility of the PS function is to address second level production support activities. This includes acting as a conduit between Applications Development staff, the user community, the Help Desk, Database Administration, Systems Administration, and Computer Operations to resolve production problems. Another responsibility of PS is the ownership of key system management processes such as Change Management and Production Acceptance. PS is also responsible for deploying new systems (applications into production) and for implementing changes to existing systems.

Communications Liaison

The number one problem in IT by far in the people category is ineffective communication practices. This is due to several reasons:

- Fast pace of technology
- Minimal staff and overabundance of projects
- Trying to do more with less
- The two primary and largest organizations within IT (Applications Development and Infrastructure Support) have two completely different charters

That is only the beginning, but most IT professionals know all of these symptoms and problems. We also know that working in IT is not an eight-hours-a-day job—unless of course you are working seven days a week. So, who has time to communicate? The PS's primary responsibility is to improve communication practices via the Production Acceptance process.

The staff's job is to ensure IT staff participation for each mission-critical application that will eventually enter the data center. This is done by following and adhering to the Production Acceptance process, which tells them when to engage the appropriate staff for key functions (e.g., Systems Administration, network dependency, database performance recommendations, project lead, user lead, training, and so on).

Each mission-critical application should have a single PS coordinator assigned to it. A coordinator may be responsible for several applications, but it is important that each critical application have a single point of accountability for coordination and communication. Every mission-critical system has a slew of individuals responsible for ensuring a successful system transition from development to production. The PS coordinator ensures that this occurs via the Production Acceptance process.

Service Level Agreements (SLAs)

Why design separate SLAs? SLAs document the support requirements and expectations between IT and their customers. The objective for IT is to manage the customer's computing requirements and expectations based on what is documented in the SLA. So much time and effort is spent by IT to design these agreements, yet rarely have we seen them be effective. After the tremendous effort undertaken to create these SLAs, they typically end up on someone's shelf in an office collecting dust. No one has the time to effectively manage this function as a fulltime responsibility, yet the process is critical.

Each mission-critical system is initiated by a group of departmental users within the business. We recommend that you incorporate this into the PS function via the Production Acceptance process. Why have two separate processes? There should *only* be one process managing a customer's mission-critical environment.

Three-Tier Support Model

This model is one of the best structures ever designed, and probably the single most important reason the mainframe-centric data centers of the past were so successful. Table 4–1 lists the major roles and responsibilities of this structure. We strongly suggest the following noteworthy caution, however, about escalating problems from the second to the third level. There should be fear instilled into second-level support staff regarding the ramifications of escalating issues to the third level. The group's goal is to do everything possible to resolve the problem internally before escalating to the senior gurus of the department. Senior Systems Administrators and senior Database Administrators are worth their weight in gold. The entire organization needs to protect this valuable resource.

The benefits from this structure are enormous:

- First and foremost, this allows senior technical staff the opportunity to architect and design a reliable, available, and serviceable infrastructure. The goal should be for first- and second-level support staff to handle 80 percent of the problems before escalation

- Skills for junior and second-level support personnel are enhanced. There is a clear career development path for technical staff. Organizations today need to breed senior technical staff within the organization as quickly as possible, and continue with their external recruitment efforts

- Better turnaround for problem resolution

- The ability to fully analyze, implement, and customize enterprise systems management solutions. This is a critical benefit because, in today's IT environment, companies are devouring system management tools but rarely have the time to fully implement them because the senior gurus are too busy resolving ninety percent of the problems that come into IT

- Stabilize both network and server environments and operations

- Efficiency in the areas of Problem Management, and so on, thereby establishing integrity

- Simplified data feeds and loads

- Assisting senior technical staff in the analysis, implementation, and customization of enterprise-wide system management tools. A huge problem in the IT industry today (started in the early 1990s), it takes at least one for each type of discipline (tape backup, security, and so on). Pair a very senior person and one junior person to work together. Once trained, junior administrators can take ownership and provide maintenance on

Table 4–1   Descriptions of Roles and Responsibilities in Three Tier Support Model

Level 1	• Monitor the systems (servers, network, peripheral devices) • Perform incremental and full backups • Provide Tape Librarian functions • Assist in the physical layout of production servers • Problem resolution • Level 1 Problem Management process; the problem is escalated to Level 2 support
Level 2	• Process design, implementation, ownership, and accountability (Production Acceptance, Change Management, etc.) • Support software installation and configuration • Perform system maintenance as required • Perform Storage Management functions • 24×7 on-call support • Participates in Disaster Recovery drills • Establish end-of-life plans to deactivate servers and applications • Monitor system and network performance • Provide online availability statistics • Define and reset standards to support mission-critical applications • Problem determination and attempted resolution. After N minutes as stated in the Problem Mgmt process, the problem will be escalated to Level 3 • Problem resolution
Level 3	• Physical location of the server, network connections, and power for all peripherals • Preventive maintenance diagnostics on all incoming equipment • Configuring the OS • Apply patches to the OS as needed • Assist Database Administration with RDBMS installations • Install any unbundled products, such as tape mgmt and disk mirroring, applying patches to unbundled products as needed • Install all required support packages, such as the console server, auto-pager, preventive maintenance routines, and so on • Support of software installation and configuration • Maintain and configure system security • Perform system maintenance as required • 24×7 on-call support • Facilitates Disaster Recovery drills • Monitor system and network performance • Tune systems for peak performance • Implement Capacity Planning • Perform security audits; monitor security access • Establish system user accounts root ownership • Define and reset standards to support mission-critical applications • Problem resolution; the buck stops here (If they cannot fix the problem, then no one can.) • Design and architect the appropriate infrastructure • Problem resolution

the tool. We can learn a couple of lessons from this engagement. First, the pairing of senior and junior staff provides a mentoring process so that less experienced staff can learn on the job, which builds overall competency and individual skill sets. Second, systems management tools are not that easy to implement and maintain, as we alluded to earlier in the book, and despite what the vendors may claim. Remember, our data shows that most companies fail to use the full potential of system management tools; therefore they do not take full advantage of their capabilities. IT needs to devote senior level resources to fully implement and customize these tools

- Assisting senior technical staff in providing junior Systems Administration functions (O/S support, hardware setup, on call support, and so on). Senior technical staff should not get bogged down with day-to-day maintenance functions. If your IT organization is going to rely on those architects and planners that report into the CIO to build an infrastructure that is a competitive advantage for the business, then guess again. There is only one group that can design, implement, and customize enterprise-wide system management solutions. Therefore, IT organizations have to relieve senior gurus from day-to-day maintenance functions by providing them with Level 2 Junior Systems Administrators

System Management Process Ownership

Key enterprise-wide system management processes (i.e., Change Management, Production Acceptance) should be centrally owned by this group. This PS staff should have accountability for the design, development, and maintenance of at least these two critical enterprise-wide processes. Among the twelve disciplines described in Rich Schiesser's book entitled *IT Systems Management*, these two are probably the most critical for ensuring RAS.

Production Gatekeepers

No system shall enter the holy temple (data center) before its time. All systems internally developed by the Applications Development organization need to adhere to an SDLC methodology before they are transitioned into production via the Production Acceptance process. The bottom line is, if you want high availability while focusing on customer service, the main ingredient is the PS function.

Problems Prevented by a PS Organization

Table 4–2 lists some of the major problems solved with a well designed, adequately staffed, and management-supported PS department. If you still believe in discarding this function from your Enterprise Infrastructure Services Organization, you may want to reconsider.

Summary

This chapter began by describing the primary responsibilities of a PS function within an IT infrastructure. We then showed that chief among these responsibilities is that of serving as a communication liaison to the various key departments within IT and to key customer departments outside of IT. Part of this communication to customers includes negotiating SLAs. Next, we discussed the critical importance of a three tier support structure, and listed many of the roles and responsibilities associated with each level of support. Finally, we concluded with a summary of the major problems that can be solved with a PS department.

Table 4–2   Problems Prevented by a Production Services Organization

Problem	Description
Ineffective Enterprise-Wide Processes	Most Infrastructure Services Organizations lack many of the key processes required to maintain RAS. The very few that have the proper processes lack centralized ownership and accountability throughout the enterprise. Ownership and accountability of critical processes (i.e., Production Acceptance and Change Management) are part of the overall PS function. If processes are ineffective or missing, then RAS is unattainable.
System Management Tools not Fully Implemented	System management solutions cannot be fully implemented and customized to effectively manage the enterprise. Senior technical staff simply do not have the time or bandwidth to do it right. In today's IT environments, they are too busy resolving production issues. Highly paid senior technical staff should not be spending most of their time resolving problems. Problem resolution should only be 20% of their job function. Senior staff should be performing strategic initiatives: • Planning and architecting a cost-effective infrastructure. • Designing and analyzing enterprise-wide system management solutions • R&D on the latest and greatest technologies PS provides second level production support functions to free up much needed cycles for senior technical staff to perform these key functions.
Poor Communication Within IT and External to IT	Ineffective communication practices run rampant between Applications Development and Infrastructure Services in just about every shop we have assessed. The key role of PS is to ensure effective communication practices via the Production Acceptance process.
RAS Does Not Exist	The PS function is the heart and soul of QA for IT. Without this function there is no RAS. PS's job is to ensure RAS. As mentioned earlier, in today's IT environment RAS does not even exist. The biggest reason for this is the demolishing of the Production Control function.
An Unstable Production Environment	IT Infrastructure Services requirements are not being addressed early on in the SDLC. Systems are being thrown over the wall into Operations. There is also very little or no communication between IT and its users. Without a PS function, and specifically a Production Acceptance process, high availability and a high level of customer service is unattainable.
Poorly Deployed New Applications	Little or no testing, no user acceptance, inadequate capacity, no operator training, no Help Desk training.

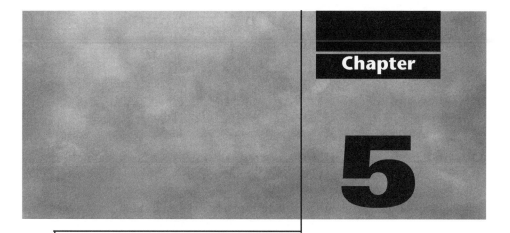

Chapter

5

The Production Acceptance Process

Introduction

No matter how well designed and well tested an application may be, the first—and often lasting—impressions that users form about that application come from how successfully it is deployed into production. Developers and Operations personnel sometimes let unnecessary obstacles take their eyes off the goal of a successful deployment. This chapter defines the process of Production Acceptance and describes many of the benefits such a process provides to a variety of groups both inside and outside of IT. The remaining sections of this chapter discuss each of the fourteen steps required to design and implement an effective Production Acceptance process.

Definition of Production Acceptance

The primary objective of systems management is to provide a consistently stable and responsive operating environment. A secondary goal is to ensure that the production systems run in a stable and responsive manner. The systems management function that addresses this challenge is *Production Acceptance*. Its formal definition is as follows.

Production Acceptance	A methodology to consistently and successfully deploy application systems into a production environment, regardless of platform.

Several key words are worth noting. While the methodology is consistent, it is not necessarily identical across all platforms. This means there are essential steps in the process for every production deployment, and then there are other steps that can be added, omitted, or modified, depending on the type of platform selected for production use.

Deploying into a production environment implies that the process is not complete until all users are fully up and running on the new system. For large applications, this could involve thousands of users phased in over several months. The term *application system* refers to any group of software programs necessary for conducting a company's business—the end-users of which are primarily, but not necessarily, in departments outside of IT. This excludes software still in development, as well as software used as tools for IT support groups.

The Benefits of a Production Acceptance Process

An effective production deployment process offers several advantages to a variety of user groups (Figure 5–1).

Executive Management

1. Quantifies total ongoing support costs prior to project start-up
2. Reduces overtime costs by identifying upgrade requirements early
3. Increases the likelihood of deploying production systems on schedule by ensuring thorough and timely testing

Infrastructure

1. Identifies initial system and network requirements early on
2. Identifies future infrastructure requirements enabling more cost- effective capacity planning
3. Identifies ongoing support requirements early on

Applications

1. Ensures that adequate network and system capacity is available for both development and production
2. Identifies desktop upgrade requirements in advance to ensure sufficient budget, resources, and time frame
3. Specifies detailed hardware and software configurations of both the development and production servers to ensure identical environments are used for testing and deployment

Suppliers

1. Involves key suppliers in the success of the project
2. Identifies and partners key suppliers with each other and with support groups
3. Provides suppliers with opportunities to suggest improvements for deployment

Customers

1. Involves customers early in the planning phase
2. Ensures customer equipment upgrades are identified early and scheduled with customer involvement
3. Ensures satisfactory user testing

Figure 5–1 Beneficiaries and benefits of Production Acceptance.

Implementing a Production Acceptance Process

Figure 5–2 lists the 14 steps necessary for implementing an effective Production Acceptance process. Along with our detailed discussion of each of these steps, we will look at actual industry experiences

```
 1. Identify an executive sponsor.
 2. Select a process owner.
 3. Solicit executive support.
 4. Assemble a Production Acceptance team.
 5. Identify and prioritize requirements.
 6. Develop policy statements.
 7. Nominate a pilot system.
 8. Design appropriate forms.
 9. Document the procedures.
10. Execute the pilot system.
11. Conduct a lessons-learned session.
12. Revise policies, procedures, and forms.
13. Formulate marketing strategy.
14. Follow up on ongoing enforcement and improvements.
```

Figure 5–2   Steps for implementing a Production Acceptance process.

(where appropriate), highlighting suggestions to pursue and obstacles to avoid.

Step 1: Identify an Executive Sponsor.

Production Acceptance is one of a handful of systems management processes that directly involve departments outside the infrastructure group. In this case, Applications Development plays a key role in making this process effective. An executive sponsor is necessary to ensure ongoing support and cooperation between these two departments. Depending on the size and scope of the IT organization, the sponsor could be the CIO, the head of the infrastructure group, or some other executive in the infrastructure.

We should note that, providing the head of the infrastructure agrees with the selection, an application manager could be an excellent sponsor. In this case, the executives from both the applications and infrastructure departments should concur on the choice of the process owner, who needs to be from the infrastructure group.

In general, the higher the level of executive sponsors the better. It should be noted that senior executives are usually more time constrained than those at lower levels, so support sessions should be well planned, straightforward, and to the point.

The executive sponsor must be a champion of the process, particularly if the shop has gone many years with no structured turnover procedure in place. He or she needs to be able to persuade other executives both inside and outside of IT to follow the lead. This individual is responsible for providing executive leadership, direction, and support for the process. The executive sponsor is also responsible for selecting the process owner, for addressing conflicts that the process owner cannot resolve, and for providing marketing assistance.

Step 2: Select a Process Owner.

One of the first responsibilities of the executive sponsor is to select the Production Acceptance process owner. The process owner should be a member of the infrastructure organization, since most of the ongoing activities of operating and supporting a new production application fall within this group. This person will be interacting frequently with programmers who developed (and will be maintaining) the system.

This continual interaction with applications makes a working knowledge of application systems an important prerequisite for the process owner. Being able to evaluate applications documentation and to communicate effectively with program developers are two additional highly recommended characteristics of a process owner. Several other medium-priority and lower-priority characteristics (shown in Table 5–1) will assist in selecting the process lead. These attributes and priorities may vary from shop to shop, but are intended to emphasize the importance of predetermining the traits that will best suit your organization.

Step 3: Solicit Executive Support.

Production Acceptance requires much cooperation and support between the Applications Development and departments providing infrastructure support. Executive support from both of these departments should be solicited to ensure that policies and decisions about the design of the process are backed up and pushed down from higher levels of management.

Table 5-1 Prioritized Characteristics for a Production Acceptance Process Owner

Characteristic	Priority
1. Knowledge of applications	High
2. Ability to evaluate documentation	High
3. Ability to communicate effectively with developers	High
4. Knowledge of company's business model	Medium
5. Ability to meet effectively with users	Medium
6. Ability to communicate effectively with IT executives	Medium
7. Ability to promote teamwork and cooperation	Medium
8. Ability to manage diversity	Medium
9. Knowledge of backup systems	Medium
10. Knowledge of database systems	Medium
11. Knowledge of desktop hardware and software	Medium
12. Knowledge of software configurations	Medium
13. Knowledge of systems software and components	Low
14. Knowledge of network software and components	Low
15. Knowledge of hardware configurations	Low

Step 4: Assemble a Production Acceptance Team.

The process owner should assemble a cross functional team to assist in developing and implementing a Production Acceptance process. The team should consist of key representatives from the development organization as well as those from Operations, Technical Support, Capacity Planning, the Help Desk, and Database Administration. In cases where the development group is larger than a few hundred programmers, multiple development representatives should participate.

It is important that all key areas within development be represented on this team to ensure support and *buy-in* for the process. Appropriate development representatives also ensure that potential obstacles to success are identified and resolved to everyone's satisfaction. An effective executive sponsor and the soliciting of executive support (Steps 1 and 3) can help to ensure proper representation.

At one company where we managed a large infrastructure group, there were over 400 programmers in the development department, grouped into the four areas of finance, engineering, manufacturing, and logistics. A representative from each of these four areas participated in the development of a Production Acceptance procedure. Each brought unique perspectives, and together they helped to ensure a successful result to the process.

Step 5: Identify and Prioritize Requirements.

Early in our careers, we participated on a number of Production Acceptance teams that fell short in providing an effective production turnover process. In looking for common causes for these failed attempts, we noticed that in almost every case there were no requirements agreed upon at the start. When there *were* requirements, they were never prioritized.

Later on, as we led our own Production Acceptance design teams, we realized that having requirements that were prioritized and agreed upon by all participants added greatly to the success of the efforts. Requirements will vary from company to company, but some are common to almost all instances. Table 5–2 lists some of the more common requirements we have witnessed in successful implementations of Production Acceptance, along with their typical priorities.

Table 5–2   Ratings of *Quality* Characteristics for Various Types of Infrastructure Process Documentation

Requirement	Priority
1. Ensure that Operations, Technical Support, Database Administration, Help Desk, and Network Services are all involved early on in implementing a new application.	High
2. Ensure capacity-gathering requirements are compatible with the Capacity Planning process.	High
3. Provide application documentation to Operations prior to production turnover.	High
4. Develop and enforce management policy statements.	High
5. Ensure adequate Help Desk support from applications during the first week of production.	Medium
6. Implement a pilot subset for very large applications.	Medium
7. Do not set up a separate Help Desk for a new application.	Medium
8. Ensure that a user test plan is developed and executed.	Medium
9. Ensure that a user acceptance plan is developed and executed.	Medium
10. Analyze daily the types and frequencies of Help Desk calls during the first two weeks of production; then weekly.	Medium
11. Leverage the use of existing tools and processes.	Medium
12. Simplify forms as much as possible for ease of use.	Low
13. Involve appropriate groups in the design and approval of forms.	Low
14. Ensure that developers estimate the type and volume of Help Desk calls during the first week of production.	Low
15. Include desktop capacity requirements.	Low
16. For systems being upgraded, ensure that all impacts to end-users are identified up front.	Low

Step 6: Develop Policy Statements.

The cross functional team should develop policy statements for a Production Acceptance process that should be developed by and approved by the executive sponsor. This will help to ensure that compliance, enforcement, and accountability will be supported by senior management and communicated to the applicable levels of staff. Figure 5–3 lists several sample policy statements.

1. All new mainframe or server-based applications are to go through the formal Production Acceptance process prior to deployment into production.
2. All major new versions of existing production applications are to go through the formal Production Acceptance process prior to deployment into production.
3. Process owner is responsible for coordinating and maintaining the Production Acceptance process and has authority to delay an application's deployment into production pending full compliance with the process.
4. Key support groups such as Operations, Technical Support, Network Services, Database Administration, and the Help Desk are to be informed about the application from its start and involved with its development as prescribed by the Production Acceptance process.
5. Development owners of applications that are deployed through the Production Acceptance process are expected to regularly update the capacity plan for their applications to ensure adequate resource support in the future.
6. Any applications deployed through the Production Acceptance process that require substantial desktop capacity upgrades are to provide specific requirements to capacity planners with sufficient lead time for planning, ordering, delivering, and installing all upgrades.

Figure 5–3   Sample policy statements.

Step 7: Nominate a Pilot System.

When a Production Acceptance process is designed and implemented, particularly in environments that have never had one, there is normally a major change in the manner by which application systems are deployed. It is usually more effective, therefore, to introduce this new method of production turnover on a smaller scale with a minimal impact pilot system. If a small system is not available as a pilot, consider putting only an initial portion of a major system through the new process.

Step 8: Design Appropriate Forms.

During the requirements step (Step 5), the cross functional team will normally discuss the quantity, types, and characteristics of forms to be used with a Production Acceptance process. We will look at some of the forms that are typically considered in this process. Figure 5–4 shows some of the most common of these forms. Some shops elect to combine some or all of these forms depending on their complexity.

Note:	
	• The capacity form is for periodic updates to resource requirements
	• The customer acceptance form is for user feedback prior to deployment
	• The Help Desk form is for anticipated calls during start-up
	• The test plan is for developers to demonstrate function and performance of the new system
	• The lessons-learned form is for follow-up and improvements after full deployment of a new system

```
1. Primary Production Acceptance form
2. Capacity Planning form
3. Customer Acceptance form
4. Help Desk form
5. Testing plan
6. Lessons-learned form
```

Figure 5–4   Lists of Production Acceptance forms.

The forms are proposed, designed, and finalized by the team. Figures 5–5, 5–6, and 5–7 show a Production Acceptance form in use by one of our clients. Specific requirements of the form will vary from shop to shop, but the form should always be simple, thorough, understandable, and accessible. Many shops today keep forms like these online via their company intranet for ease of use and access.

Step 9: Document the Procedures.

The documentation of any systems management process is important, but it is especially so in the case of Production Acceptance because such a large number of developers will be using it. The documentation for these procedures must be effective and accessible. Many shops develop excellent processes but fail to document them adequately. After an initially successful implementation of the process, many of these procedures become unused due to lack of documentation, particularly as new staff members who are unfamiliar with the process attempt to use it.

Some documentation is usually better than none at all, but adding value and quality to it increases the likelihood of the proper use of the process it details. Evaluating the quality of documentation can easily become a very subjective activity. Few techniques exist to objectively quantify the quality and value of process documentation. That is why the following methodology is so unique and beneficial. We developed this approach over several years while working with many clients who were struggling with ways to determine both the quality and the value of their process documentation.

The purpose of evaluating the *quality* of content is to show to what degree the material is suitable for use. The purpose of evaluating its *value* is to show how important the documentation is to the support of the process and how important the process is to the support of the business. The quality of the content of documentation is evaluated with ten common characteristics of usability. Figure 5–8 lists these characteristics of quality of content and gives a definition of each.

The value of the documentation is next evaluated with five common characteristics of importance. Figure 5–9 lists these characteristics of value and gives a definition of each.

The characteristic in both the quality and value figures were rated on a 0 to 3 scale based on the degree to which elements of each characteristic were met. Table 5–3 describes these ratings and their meanings.

Benefits of the Methodology to Evaluate Process Documentation

There are three major benefits to this method of documentation evaluation. The first is that it gives a snapshot of the quality of existing documentation at that point in time, particularly documentation of high value. If improvements are made to the materials that result in new ratings, then they can be compared to the current rating.

The second benefit is that this method gives us the ability to customize the criteria for quality and value of documentation to reflect changes in priority, strategy, or direction. In this way, the methodology remains applicable regardless of the specific criteria used. The third benefit of this method is that it allows comparisons between different types of processes within an infrastructure using the same standard of measure.

A client at a satellite broadcasting company recently asked us to evaluate a variety of their infrastructure process documentation. Table 5–4 lists the thirty-two pieces of documentation that we assessed and shows the wide diversity of material involved in the review.

Table 5–5 lists the results of assessing the *quality* characteristics of each piece of documentation and shows the variety of numerical totals that resulted.

Table 5–6 lists the results of assessing the value characteristics for each of the same pieces of documentation. Next, we will discuss how these two pieces of information can be used together to indicate which pieces of documentation should be improved upon first

Once both the quality and value characteristics are evaluated, the two sets of attributes can be shown on a quality/value matrix (see Figure 5–10). Quality ratings are shown along the horizontal axis increasing to the right. Value ratings are shown along the vertical axis increasing as it ascends. Each axis is scaled from the lowest quality and value ratings up to the maximum possible. The benefit of such a matrix is that it depicts both the value and quality of each piece of documentation on a single chart.

The matrix is then divided into four quadrants. Points in the upper right quadrant (1) represent documentation that is both high in value and high in quality. This is the desired place to be, and constitutes excellent documentation that requires little or no improvement and only periodic reviews to ensure continued high quality. Points in the lower right quadrant (2) signify material that is high in quality but has a lower value to a particular infrastructure. Documentation in this area is generally rated as good but could be improved.

The lower left quadrant (3) represents documentation that is relatively low in both value and quality. Material in this area is designated as only *fair* and needs to be improved in quality. Since the value is low, improvements are suggested on a time-permitting basis. Points in the upper left quadrant (4) indicate documentation that is high in value but low in quality. Documentation in this area is considered to be at the greatest risk since it represents material that is of particular importance to this organization but is of poor quality. Documentation in this quarter of the matrix should be improved as soon as possible to prevent adverse impact to processes, procedures, and services.

Table 5–7 shows the combinations of the totals of the quality ratings from Table 5–5 and the totals of the value ratings from Table 5–6. Each entry is again numbered with the identifiers used in Table 5–4. Figure 5–11 shows the quality/value matrix populated with the identifiers of each piece of documentation in their appropriate quadrants. This depiction clearly shows which pieces of documentation need the greatest improvement in the most urgent manner.

Those identifiers closest to the upper left corner of quadrant four are in the greatest need of quick improvement because they are of the highest value to the organization and yet have the lowest level of quality. In this specific evaluation, it happens to be the documentation for Disaster Recovery denoted by Identifier 22. Once these particular pieces of documentation are identified in the populated quality/value matrix, Table 5–7 can be used to determine which specific characteristics of documentation quality need to be improved most.

Software technologies, in the form of statistical analysis programs that integrate with any number of graphical presentation products, provide the means to automate the generation of these displays and reports.

Step 10: Execute the Pilot System.

With a pilot system identified, forms designed, and procedures in place, it is time to execute the pilot system. User testing and acceptance plays a major role in this step, as does the involvement of support groups such as Technical Support, Systems Administration, and the Help Desk.

Step 11: Conduct a Lessons-Learned Session.

In this step, the process owner conducts a thorough, candid, lessons-learned session with key participants involved in executing the pilot system. Participants should include representatives from the user community, development area, support staff, and Help Desk.

Production Acceptance Request Form
Part One: Actions Required at Time of Project Approval
I. General Information about the Application

Customer/Supplier Information *(To be completed by the Project Manager)*
Full system name/acronym_____
Brief description of the system_____
_____

Current Date _____ Planned Pilot Date _____Full Deployment Date_____
Risk Assessment and
Analysis_____
_____ Mission Critical (Yes/No)_____ Prty (A/B)_____
Prim Proj Mgr _____Alt Proj Mgr _____IT Dept_____
Prim Cust Contact _____Alt Cust Contact _____Cust Dept_____
Prim Ops Support _____Alt Ops Support _____Soln Ctr Rep_____

Service Level Information *(To be completed by the Project Manager)*
Tech Ctr Hrs of Oprtn _____Soln Ctr Hrs of Oprtn_____ Monitoring Hrs_____
Expected prime-shift % avail/wk: _____ Expected off-shift % avail/wk _____
For _____type transactions, expected response time is_____
For _____type transactions, expected response time is_____
Batch requirements _____

Minimum System Requirements *(To be completed by the Project Manager)*
DB System _____ Appl Vendor(if applicable)_____ ApplLang_____
Server Platform _____ Client Platform _____

Actual Development and Production Environment
(To be completed by Manager of Systems Administration)
DB System, Ver/Rel _____ Appl Vendor, Ver/Rel (if applicable)_____
Server O/S Ver/Rel _____ Dev Hostname_____ Prod Hostname_____
List any dependencies between server O/S, DB, and appl ver/rel _____
List any differences between Dev & Prod server, O/S,DB, appl, utilities, etc.
_____

Local Area Network Architecture *(To be completed by the Manager of Network Operations)*
Server Topology Required (10BaseT/100BaseT/FDDI/GB-Fiber/Other)
_____
Client Topology Required (10BaseT/100BaseT/FDDI/GB-Fiber/Other)
_____
Protocols Required (TCPIP/Other) _____ Estimated Bandwidth_____
Ntwk Class: On-air_____ Business_____ Internet Access (Yes/No)_____
Prod Loc: Data Ctr_____ Other_____ Switch Location_____
Wide Area Network Architecture *(To be completed by the Manager of Network Operations)*
Comments_____
_____

Figure 5–5   Sample Production Acceptance form, part I.

Production Acceptance Request Form
Part One: Actions Required at Time of Project Approval

II. Capacity, Support, and Costs

	Time at Start-Up	6 Mos after Start-Up	12 Mos after Start-Up

Application Usage Information *(To be completed by the Project Manager)*

	Time at Start-Up	6 Mos after Start-Up	12 Mos after Start-Up
1. Concurrent LAN users	_____	_____	_____
2. Total LAN users	_____	_____	_____
3. Concurrent WAN users	_____	_____	_____
4. Total WAN users	_____	_____	_____
5. Concurrent remote users	_____	_____	_____
6. Total remote users	_____	_____	_____
7. Total concurrent users (sum of 1, 3, 5)	_____	_____	_____
8. Total overall users (sum of 2, 4, 6)	_____	_____	_____

Application Resource Information *(To be completed by the Project Manager)*

1. Disk storage (GB)	_____	_____	_____
2. New/upgraded desktops	_____	_____	_____
3. Peak update transactions/hour	_____	_____	_____
4. Peak inquiry transactions/hour	_____	_____	_____
5. Peak data throughput/hour	_____	_____	_____
6. Avg. data throughput/hour	_____	_____	_____

Technical Center Capacity Requirements *(To be completed by the Manager of Systems Administration)*

1. Additional server required	_____	_____	_____
2. Type of server required	_____	_____	_____
3. Server processor upgrades	_____	_____	_____
4. Server memory upgrades	_____	_____	_____
5. Server software upgrades	_____	_____	_____
6. Disk resource upgrades	_____	_____	_____
7. Tape resource upgrades	_____	_____	_____
8. Backup media required	_____	_____	_____
9. Physical floor space	_____	_____	_____
10. Racks, cabinets, furniture	_____	_____	_____
11. Facilities (electrical, a/c, etc.)	_____	_____	_____

Operations Support Requirements *(To be completed by the Manager of Systems Administration)*

1. FTE Computer Operator	_____	_____	_____
2. FTE Systems Administrator	_____	_____	_____
3. FTE Database Administrator	_____	_____	_____
4. FTE Network Operator	_____	_____	_____
5. FTE Call Center Analyst	_____	_____	_____

_____ Project Manager Date   _____ Customer Contact Date   _____ Primary Operations Support Date

_____ Systems Administrators Manager Date   _____ Network Operations Manager Date

_____ Solution Center Manager Date

Figure 5–5   Sample Production Acceptance form, part I. (Continued)

Production Acceptance Request Form
Part Two: Actions Required during Week Prior to Start-Up

	No	In Progress	Yes	N/A
I. Application Usage Information *(from Project Manager)*				
System Architecture Diagram	___	___	___	___
System Flow Diagram	___	___	___	___
Operator Run Instructions	___	___	___	___
Backup Requirements	___	___	___	___
Disaster Recovery Requirements	___	___	___	___
Project Plan with All Current Infrastructure	___	___	___	___
User Acceptance Test Plans	___	___	___	___
User Guide	___	___	___	___
DBA Documents	___	___	___	___
(data model, dictionary, scripts, etc.)				
II. Status of Testing *(from Project Manager)*				
Unit Tests	___	___	___	___
Systems Tests	___	___	___	___
Integration Tests (when applicable)	___	___	___	___
Regression Tests (when applicable)	___	___	___	___
Stress Tests	___	___	___	___
User Acceptance Tests	___	___	___	___
Parallel Tests	___	___	___	___
III. Training Plans *(from Project Manager)*				
Operations Support Training	___	___	___	___
Solution Center Training	___	___	___	___
User Training	___	___	___	___

_____ _____   _____ _____   _____ _____
Project Manager   Date   Customer Contact Date   Primary Operations Support Date

_____ _____   _____ _____
Systems Administrators Manager Date   Network Operations Manager Date

_____ _____
Solution Center Manager   Date

Figure 5–6 Sample Production Acceptance form, part II.

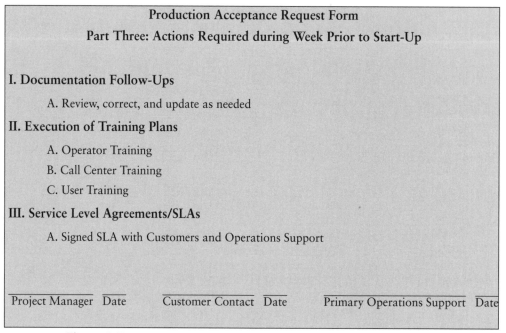

Figure 5–7   Sample Production Acceptance form, part III.

Step 12: Revise Policies, Procedures, and Forms.

The recommendations resulting from the lessons-learned session may include revisions to policies, procedures, forms, test plans, and training techniques for users and support staff. These revisions should be agreed to by the entire cross functional team and implemented prior to full deployment.

Step 13: Formulate Marketing Strategy.

Regardless of how thoroughly and effectively a cross functional team designs a Production Acceptance process, it does little good if it is not supported and applied by development groups. Once the final policies, procedures, and forms are in place, the process owner and design team should formulate and implement a marketing strategy. The marketing plan should include the benefits of using the process, the active support of the executive sponsor and peers, examples of any quick wins as evidenced by the pilot system, and testimonials from users, Help Desk personnel, and support staff.

1. **Ownership**   This characteristic rates the degree to which the three key ownership roles—process owner, documentation custodian, and technical writer—are clearly identified, understood, and supported. For some processes, the same individual may have all three roles. In most cases, the documentation custodian maintains the process documentation and reports to the process owner.
2. **Readability**   This characteristic rates the clarity and simplicity of the written documentation. Items evaluated include use of common words, terms, and phrases; correct spelling; proper use of grammar; and minimal use of acronyms, along with explanations of those that are used but not widely known. This characteristic especially looks at how well the level of the material matches the skill and experience level of the audience.
3. **Accuracy**   This characteristic rates the technical accuracy of the material.
4. **Thoroughness**   This characteristic rates how well the documentation has succeeded in including all relevant information.
5. **Format**   This characteristic rates the overall organization of the material; how easy it is to follow; how well it keeps a consistent level of technical depth; to what degree it is documenting and describing an actual process rather than merely duplicating tables, spreadsheets, and metrics.
6. **Accessibility**   This characteristic rates the ease or difficulty of accessibility.
7. **Currency**   This characteristic rates to what degree the current version of the documentation is up to date and the frequency with which it is kept current.
8. **Ease of Update**   This characteristic rates the relative ease or difficulty with which the documentation can be updated, including revision dates and distribution of new versions.
9. **Effectiveness**   This characteristic rates the overall usability of the documentation including the use of appropriate examples, graphics, color coding, use on multiple platforms, and compliance with existing standards if available.
10. **Accountability**   This characteristic rates to what degree the documentation is being read, understood, and effectively used; all appropriate users are identified and held accountable for proper use of the documentation.

Figure 5–8   Types of infrastructure documentation evaluated for quality and value.

1. **Criticality of the Process**   This characteristic describes how critical the process described by this documentation is to the successful business of the company.
2. **Frequency of Use**   This characteristic describes how frequently the documentation is used or referenced.
3. **Number of Users**   This characteristic describes the approximate number of personnel who will likely want or need to use this documentation.
4. **Variety of Users**   This characteristic describes the variety of different functional areas or skill levels of personnel who will use this documentation.
5. **Impact of Nonuse**   This characteristic describes the level of adverse impact that is likely to occur if the documentation is not used properly.

Figure 5–9   Documentation quality characteristics and definitions.

Table 5-3 Rating Quality and Value Characteristics of Documentation

Ratings are either 0, 1, 2, or 3, and are applied as follows:

0 None or an insignificant amount of the characteristic has been met.
1 A small portion of the characteristic has been met.
2 A significant, though not the entire, portion of the characteristic has been met or is present.
3 All aspects of the characteristic have been met or are present.

Table 5-4 Ratings of Quality Characteristics for Various Types of Infrastructure

Number	Description of Documentation
1	Procedure for logging all calls
2	Method for prioritizing calls
3	Determining ownership of problems
4	How to escalate problems
5	Resolution status of problems
6	Trending analysis from viewer
7	Problem Management performance reports
8	Responsibilities of Help Desk staff
9	User feedback procedures
10	Use of training plans
11	Analysis of cell phone invoices
12	Analysis of monthly cost trending
13	VMS/UNIX initiation procedures
14	New equipment planning request
15	Use of site scan tool
16	Monthly review of vendor performance
17	Change Management procedures
18	Charter of domain architecture teams
19	Monthly IT business review
20	Submitting request for service form
21	Administration of SLAs
22	Disaster Recovery plan
23	Application support
24	Work initiation process
25	SDLC
26	Project management procedures
27	Production Acceptance process
28	Data center administration
29	Backup and restore procedures
30	Production scheduling process
31	Network and server Operations
32	File transfer procedures

Table 5-5 Ratings of *Quality* Characteristics for Various Types of Infrastructure Process Documentation

Documentation	OWNERSHIP	READABILITY	ACCURACY	THOROUGHNESS	FORMAT	ACCESSIBILITY	CURRENCY	UPDATABILITY	EFFECTIVENESS	ACCOUNTABILITY	TOTALS
17. Change Management	3	3	3	2	3	2	3	3	3	3	28
1. Logging Calls	3	3	3	3	2	3	3	2	3	2	27
2. Prioritizing Calls	3	3	3	3	2	3	3	2	3	2	27
24. Work Initiation	3	3	2	3	3	2	3	3	3	2	27
4. Escalation	3	3	3	3	2	2	2	3	3	2	26
8. Resp. Help Desk Staff	2	3	3	3	3	2	3	2	3	2	26
14. New Equip. Planning	3	2	3	3	2	3	3	2	2	3	26
20. Request for Service	3	3	3	3	3	2	3	2	2	2	26
29. Backups/Restores	2	2	3	3	3	3	3	2	3	2	26
3. Ownership of Problems	2	3	2	3	2	3	3	2	3	2	25
12. Monthly Cost Trending	3	2	3	3	2	2	3	3	3	1	25
25. SDLC	2	3	2	2	3	2	3	3	2	2	25
26. Project Management	2	3	2	2	3	2	3	3	2	2	25
9. User Feedback	3	3	2	2	2	3	2	2	2	3	24
13. VMS/Unix Procedures	2	3	3	3	2	2	2	3	2	2	24
15. Site Scan Tool	2	3	3	3	2	2	3	2	2	2	24
23. Application Support	3	3	3	2	2	2	2	3	2	2	24
32. File Transfers	2	3	2	3	3	3	2	2	2	2	24
7. Prob. Mgmt. Perf. Report	2	2	3	2	2	2	3	3	2	2	23
16. Monthly Vendor Review	2	2	3	2	2	2	3	3	2	2	23
19. Monthly IT Bus. Review	3	3	3	2	1	1	3	3	2	2	23
28. Data Ctr. Administrative	2	3	2	3	3	3	1	2	2	2	23
11. Cell Phone Invoices	3	2	3	3	1	1	3	2	2	2	22
5. Resolution of Problems	2	3	2	2	2	3	3	3	2	1	21
18. Domain Arch. Teams	2	3	3	1	2	2	2	1	2	2	21
27. Production Acceptance	2	3	2	2	2	2	2	2	2	2	21
30. Prod. Sched./Processing	2	3	1	2	3	3	1	2	2	2	21
31. Network/Server Ops.	2	3	1	2	3	3	1	2	2	2	21
6. Trending Analysis	2	2	2	2	1	2	3	2	2	2	20
10. Training Plans	1	3	2	1	2	2	2	2	2	1	18
21. SLA Administration	1	3	2	2	2	1	2	2	2	1	18
22. Disaster Recovery	3	3	2	1	1	1	1	2	2	2	18

Table 5-6 Ratings of *Value* Characteristics for Various Types of Infrastructure Process Documentation

Documentation	CRITICALITY	FREQUENCY	USER NUMBER	USER VARIETY	IMPACT	TOTALS
17. Change Management	3	3	3	3	3	15
4. Escalation	3	3	2	3	3	14
22. Disaster Recovery	3	2	3	3	3	14
27. Production Acceptance	3	2	3	3	3	14
29. Backups/Restores	3	3	3	2	3	14
32. File Transfers	3	3	3	3	2	14
2. Prioritizing Calls	2	3	2	3	3	13
3. Ownership of Problems	2	3	2	3	3	13
9. User Feedback	2	3	3	3	2	13
18. Domain Arch. Teams	2	3	2	3	3	13
19. Monthly IT Business Review	3	2	2	3	3	13
20. Request for Service	2	3	3	3	2	13
21. SLA Administration	2	3	3	3	1	13
30. Production Scheduling/Processing	3	3	2	2	3	13
31. Network/Server Operations	3	2	2	3	3	13
5. Resolution Status	2	3	2	3	2	12
15. Site Scan Tool	3	2	2	2	3	12
23. Application Support	3	2	2	2	3	12
24. Work Intitiation	2	2	3	3	2	12
25. SDLC	2	2	3	3	2	12
26. Project Management	2	2	3	3	2	12
1. Logging Calls	2	3	2	2	2	11
6. Trending Analysis	2	2	2	3	2	11
7. Problem Mgmt. Perf. Reports	2	2	2	3	2	11
11. Cell Phone Invoices	1	3	3	3	1	11
12. Monthly Cost Trending	2	2	2	3	2	11
13. VMS/Unix Procedures	3	1	2	2	3	11
16. Monthly Vendor Review	2	2	2	3	2	11
10. Training Plans	3	1	2	1	3	10
8. Responsibilities of Help Desk Staff	2	1	2	1	3	9
14. New Equip. Planning	2	1	2	2	2	9
28. Data Center Administrative	2	2	2	2	1	9

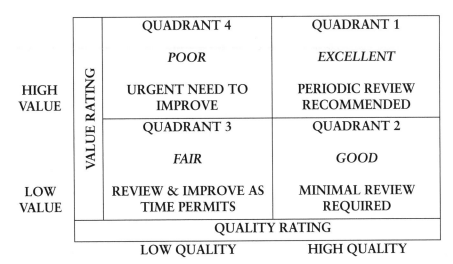

Figure 5–10   Quality/Value matrix.

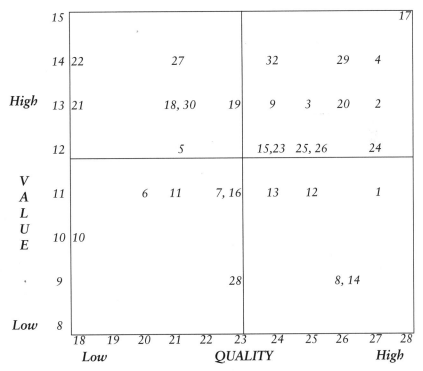

Figure 5–11   Populated quality/value matrix.

Table 5-7 Quality and Value Ratings

No.	Documentation	Quality	Value	Quad
17	Change Management	28	15	1
4	Escalation	26	14	1
2	Prioritizing Calls	27	13	1
24	Work Initiation	27	12	1
20	Request for Service	26	13	1
3	Ownership of Problems	25	13	1
25	SDLC	25	12	1
26	Project Management	25	12	1
9	User Feedback	24	13	1
15	Site Scan Tool	24	12	1
12	Monthly Cost Trending	24	12	1
23	Application Support	26	14	1
29	Backups/Restores	24	14	1
32	File Transfers	27	11	1
13	VMS/Unix Procedures	26	9	1
1	Logging Calls	26	9	1
8	Resp. Help Desk Staff	25	11	2
14	New Equipment Planning	24	11	2
12	Monthly Cost Trending	23	11	2
16	Monthly Vendor Review	23	11	2
11	Cell Phone Invoices	22	11	3
28	Data Ctr. Administrative	23	9	3
6	Trending Analysis (C/V)	20	11	3
10	Training Plans	18	10	3
27	Production Acceptance	21	14	3
19	Monthly IT Bus. Review	23	13	3
18	Domain Arch. Teams	21	13	4
30	Prod. Sched./Processing	21	13	4
31	Network/Server Ops.	21	13	4
5	Resolution Status	21	12	4
21	SLA Administration	18	13	4
22	Disaster Recovery	18	14	4

Step 14: Follow up for Ongoing Enforcement and Improvements.

Improvement processes, such as Production Acceptance, often enjoy much initial support and enthusiasm, but that sometimes becomes short-lived. Changing priorities, conflicting schedules, budget constraints, turnover of staff or management, lack of adequate resources, and a general reluctance to adopt radically new procedures all contribute to the de-emphasis and avoidance of novel processes. One of the best ways to ensure ongoing support and consistent use is to follow up with reviews, postmortems, and lessons learned to constantly improve the overall quality, enforcement, and effectiveness of the process.

Full Deployment of a New Application

By this point, the Production Acceptance process should be designed, approved, documented, tested, and implemented. So, when does the new application become deployed? The answer to that is that the process of developing the process does not specifically include the deployment of a new application. When the Production Acceptance process is applied, it will include the use of the form described in Table 5–5 that includes all of the activities leading up to the actual deployment. In other words, if all of the tasks outlined by the form in Table 5–5 are completed on time for any new application, its successful deployment is all but guaranteed.

One of the key aspects of this entire process is the early involvement of the infrastructure group. The development manager who owns the new application should notify and involve the Production Acceptance process owner as soon as a new application is approved. This ensures infrastructure personnel and support staff are given adequate lead time to plan, coordinate, and implement the required resources and training prior to deployment. Just as important is the follow-up and lessons-learned portion of the process, which usually occurs two to three weeks after initial deployment.

Distinguishing New Applications from New Versions of Existing Applications

Users of a new process understandably will have questions about when and how to apply it. One of the most frequent questions we hear asked about Production Acceptance is: Should it be used only for new applications, or is it for new versions of existing applications as well? The answer lies in the overall objective of the process, which is to consistently and successfully deploy application systems into production.

A new version of an existing application will often have major changes that impact customers and infrastructure groups alike. In this case, deploying it into production will be very similar to deploying a new application. Test plans should be developed, customer acceptance pilots should be formulated, and capacity requirements should be identified well in advance. The guideline for deciding when to use Production Acceptance is this: Determine how different the new version of the system is from its predecessor. If users, support staff, and Help Desk personnel are likely to experience even moderate impact from a new version of an existing application, then the Production Acceptance process should be used.

Distinguishing Production Acceptance from Change Management

Another question we frequently hear is: How does one distinguish Production Acceptance from Change Management, since both seem to be handling software changes? The answer is that Production Acceptance is a special type of change that involves many more elements than the typical software modification. Capacity forecasts, resource requirements, customer sign-offs, Help Desk training, and close initial monitoring by developers are just some of the usual aspects of Production Acceptance that are normally not associated with Change Management. The other obvious difference between the two processes is that, while Production Acceptance is involved solely with deploying application software into production, Change Management covers a wide range of activities outside of production software such as hardware, networks, desktops, and facilities.

Assessing an Infrastructure's Production Acceptance Process

Over the years, many clients have asked us for a quick and simple method to evaluate the quality, efficiency, and effectiveness of their Production Acceptance processes. In response to these requests, we developed the Production Acceptance assessment worksheet shown in Figure 5–12. Process owners and their managers collaborate with other appropriate individuals to fill out this form. Along the left-hand column are 10 categories of characteristics about a process. The degree to which each of these characteristics is put to use in designing and managing a process is a good measure of its relative robustness.

The categories that assess the overall quality of a process are executive support, process owner, and process documentation. Categories assessing the overall efficiency of a process consist of supplier involvement, process metrics, process integration, and streamlining/automation. The categories used to assess effectiveness include customer involvement, service metrics, and the training of staff.

The evaluation of each category is a very simple procedure. The relative degree to which the characteristics within each category are present and being used is rated on a scale of 0 to 3, with 0 indicating no presence and 3 being a large presence of the characteristic. For example, suppose the executive sponsor for the Production Acceptance process demonstrated some initial support for the process by carefully selecting and coaching the process owner. However, presume that over time this same executive showed no interest in analyzing trending reports or holding direct report managers accountable for outages. We would consequently rate the overall degree to which this executive showed support for this process as little and rate it a 1 on the scale of 0 to 3. On the other hand, if the process owner actively engages key customers in the design and use of the process, particularly as it pertains to availability metrics and SLAs, we would rate that category a 3.

Each of the categories is similarly rated as shown in Figure 5–12. Obviously, a single column could be used record the ratings of each category; however, if we format separate columns for each of the four possible scores, categories scoring the lowest and highest ratings stand out visually. We have filled in sample responses for each of the categories to show how the entire assessment might work. We now sum the numerical scores within each column. In our sample worksheet this totals to 0+4+6+3=13. This total is then divided by the maximum possible rating of 30 for an assessment score of 43%.

Apart from its obvious value of quantifying areas of strength and weakness for a given process, this rating provides two other significant benefits to an infrastructure. One is that it serves as a baseline benchmark from which future process refinements can be quantitatively measured and compared. The second is that the score of this particular process can be compared to those of other infrastructure processes to determine which ones need most attention.

In our experience, many infrastructures do not attribute the same amount of importance to each of the 10 categories within a process, just as they do not all associate the same degree of value to all systems management processes. We refined the assessment worksheet to account for this uneven distribution of category significance, allowing weights to be assigned to each of the categories. The weights range from 1 for least important to 5 for most important, with a default of 3.

Figure 5–13 demonstrates how this works. We provide sample weights for each of the rated categories from our sample in Figure 5–12. The weight for each category is multiplied by its rating to produce a final score. For example, the executive support category is weighted at 5 and rated at 1 for a final score of 5. We generate scores for the other nine categories in a similar manner and sum up the numbers in each column. In our sample worksheet, the weights add up to 32, the ratings add up to 13 as before, and the new scores add up to 45.

The overall weighted assessment score is calculated by dividing this final score of 45 by the Maximum Weighted Score (MWS). By definition, the MWS will vary from process to process, and from shop to shop, since it reflects the specific weighting of categories tailored to a given environment. The MWS is the product of the sum of the ten weights multiplied by 3, the maximum rating for any category. In our example, the sum of the ten weights is 32, so our MWS = 45 / (32×3) = 45/96 = 47%.

Your next question could well be this: Why is the overall weighted assessment score of 47% higher than the nonweighted assessment score of 43%, and what is the significance of this? The answer to the first question is quantitative and to the second one, qualitative. The weighted score will be higher whenever categories with high weights receive high ratings or categories with low weights receive low ratings. When the reverse occurs, the weighted score will be lower than the nonweighted one. In this case, the categories of customer involvement, supplier involvement, and service metrics were given the maximum weights and scored high on the ratings, resulting in a higher overall score.

The significance of this is that a weighted score will reflect a more accurate assessment of a process because each category is assigned a customized weight. The more frequently the weight deviates from the default value of 3, the greater the difference will be between the weighted and nonweighted values.

Measuring and Streamlining the Production Acceptance Process

We can measure and streamline the Production Acceptance process with the help of the assessment worksheet shown in Figure 5–12. We can measure the effectiveness of a Production Acceptance process with service metrics such as the amount of positive feedback from users and the number of calls to the Help Desk immediately after deployment. Process metrics—such as the frequency and duration of delays to deployment and the accuracy and timeliness of documentation and training—help us gauge the efficiency of the process. And we can streamline the Production Acceptance process by automating certain actions such as the documentation of a new application and online training for it by means of the intranet.

Summary

Production Acceptance is the first systems management process we have looked at that significantly involves other departments and for which we offer a structured methodology to develop its procedures. We began with a formal definition of Production Acceptance followed by a summary of the 14 steps necessary to implement this process successfully.

We then discussed each of the 14 steps in detail and included recommended attributes for a Production Acceptance process owner, examples of prioritized requirements and policy statements, and a sample of a Production Acceptance process form. We concluded this chapter by explaining the differences between Production Acceptance of new applications versus that of new versions of existing applications and the Change Management process, plus a discussion of self-assessment worksheets for a Production Acceptance process.

Production Acceptance Process—Assessment Worksheet					
Process Owner_____ Owner's Manager _____ Date_____					
Category	Questions for Production Acceptance	None	Small	Med	Lg
Executive Support	To what degree does the executive sponsor show support for the Production Acceptance process with actions such as engaging development managers and their staffs in this process?		1		
Process Owner	To what degree does the process owner exhibit desirable traits and understand Applications Development and deployment?				3
Customer Involvement	To what degree are key customers—especially from Development, Operations, and the Help Desk—involved in the design and use of the process.			2	
Supplier Involvement	To what degree are key suppliers, such as third-party vendors, trainers, and technical writers, involved in the design of the process?		1		
Service Metrics	To what degree are service metrics analyzed for trends, such as the amount of positive feedback from users and the number of calls to the Help Desk immediately after deployment?			2	
Process Metrics	To what degree are process metrics analyzed for trends such as the frequency and duration of delays to deployment and the accuracy and timelines of documentation and training?	0			
Process Integration	To what degree is the Production Acceptance process integrated with other processes and tools such as Change Management and Problem Management?		1		
Streamlining Automation	To what degree is the Production Acceptance process streamlined by automating actions such as the documentation of a new application and online training for it by means of the intranet?	0			
Training of Staff	To what degree is the staff cross-trained on the Production Acceptance process, and how is the effectiveness of the training verified?			2	
Process Documentation	To what degree is the quality and value of Production Acceptance documentation measured and maintained?		1		
	Totals	0	4	6	3
Grand Total = 13					
Nonweighted Assessment Score = 13/30 = 43%					

Figure 5–12   Sample assessment worksheet for Production Acceptance process.

Production Acceptance Process—Assessment Worksheet					
Process Owner_____ Owner's Manager _____ Date_____					
Category	Questions for Production Acceptance	Wgt.	Rating	Score
Process Owner	To what degree are key customers—especially from Development, Operations, and the Help Desk—involved in the design and use of the process.	3	3	9
Customer Involvement	To what degree does the process owner exhibit desirable traits and understand Applications Development and deployment?	5	2	10
Supplier Involvement	To what degree are key suppliers, such as third-party vendors, trainers, and technical writers, involved in the design of the process?	1	1	1
Service Metrics	To what degree are service metrics analyzed for trends, such as the amount of positive feedback from users and the number of calls to the Help Desk immediately after deployment?	3	2	6
Process Metrics	To what degree are process metrics analyzed for trends, such as the frequency and duration of delays to deployment and the accuracy and timelines of documentation and training?	3	0	0
Process Integration	To what degree is the Production Acceptance process integrated with other processes and tools, such as Change Management and Problem Management?	1	1	1
Streamlining Automation	To what degree is the Production Acceptance process streamlined by automating actions, such as the documentation of a new application and online training for it by means of the intranet?	3	0	0
Training of Staff	To what degree is the staff cross-trained on the Production Acceptance process, and how is the effectiveness of the training verified?	5	2	10
Process Documentation	To what degree is the quality and value of Production Acceptance documentation measured and maintained?	3	1	3
	Totals	32	13	45

Figure 5–13   Sample assessment worksheet for Production Acceptance process with weighting factors.

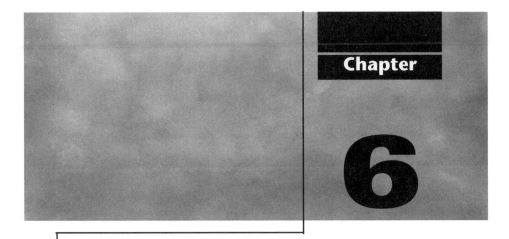

Case Studies

Introduction

All the theory in the world about designing world class infrastructures is of little use if it cannot be applied to real-life environments. In this chapter, we present actual applications of infrastructure processes in general, and of the Production Acceptance process in particular. All of the material in this section is taken from work involving Production Services (PS) that we performed over the past several years at seven separate companies. We place emphasis on the Production Acceptance process of a PS department. The companies vary significantly in size, age, industry, orientation, and IT maturity. As a result, they offer a wide diversity of industry experiences in how companies recognize, support, and improve the quality of their PS environments.

In addition to the general company attributes mentioned above, we describe several key IT characteristics of each firm. This is to show both the amount and range of diversity in the IT departments of these organizations. Each company is then discussed in more detail with emphasis on the particular strengths and weaknesses of its approach to infrastructure processes. We include one of the unique features of this book in this discussion: a completed assessment worksheet for measuring the relative quality and robustness of each company's Production Acceptance process. Last, we summarize and compare the attributes, and the relative strengths, weaknesses, and lessons learned from each of the seven companies studied.

The Seven Companies Selected

We selected seven companies based on our familiarity with each firm as either a client of our professional services, or as one whose infrastructure we personally managed. We feel fortunate that these companies provided such a wide variety of IT environments. To really gain insight from studying the relative strengths and weaknesses of numerous PS departments, it is helpful to learn from a variety of IT environments.

The seven companies from which we draw our individual experiences could not be more diverse. They each consisted primarily of one of the four major platform environments: mainframe, midrange, client-server, or Web-enabled. No two were in the same industry. They covered a wide spectrum of businesses that included aerospace, broadcast content, motion pictures, defense contracting, dotcom e-tailor, broadcast delivery, and financial services.

The age of the oldest company (50 years) was more than 10 times the age of the youngest one. Even more striking was the variation by a factor of one thousand for the number of total employees, and the number of IT employees specifically. Despite the diversity of these companies, they all had production applications to deploy, operate, maintain, and manage. They all shared a common production goal to run these systems as reliably and as efficiently as possible. The degree to which they accomplished that goal varied almost as widely as the environments that described them. Studying what each of these companies did well (or not so well) when managing their applications provides important lessons as to how to implement a truly world class PS department.

Types of Attributes

In setting out to study and analyze the PS function of these companies, we first identified attributes of each company that fell into one of three categories: business oriented, IT oriented, and PS oriented.

- The business-oriented attributes were high-level qualifiers and consisted of the type of industry of the company, the total number of its employees at the time we performed our work, and the number of years it had been in business. As mentioned previously, these companies represented a wide variety of industries, including manufacturing, high technology, entertainment, and services. The largest company employed some 80,000 workers while the smallest had 75. The average size was 17,300. The age of the companies similarly spanned a wide range with the oldest being in existence for over 70 years, the youngest for four years, and the average being exactly 31

- One of the IT-oriented characteristics we used was the number of IT employees, with a range from 25 up to 2000, and an average of 457. The largest IT department in our sample is skewing the data slightly because the average would be a more reasonable 200 with it removed. The other IT attribute we selected was the number of processors by platform. This provided us a good mix both in terms of numbers of processors and the types of platforms

- The PS-oriented attributes described such characteristics as the total number of production applications in a company's inventory, the number deployed per month, whether a PS department even existed, and if so, to which department it reported

Figure 6–1 lists all of these attributes for each of the seven companies. We identify these seven firms simply as Company A, Company B, and so on through Company G. A few observations are worth noting, aside from the obvious diversity of the companies. One is that the size of the company does not necessarily dictate the size of the IT department. For example, Company A has 80,000 employees, with 400 of them in IT, while Company D has 30,000 workers with 2,000 of them in IT. This is because Company A has many manufacturing workers not directly tied to IT, whereas Company D has major defense programs requiring huge IT investments.

Attributes	Company A	Company B	Company C	Company D	Company E	Company F	Company G
Industry	Aero-space	Broadcast Content	Motion Pictures	Defense Contracting	Dot-com E-tailor	Broadcast Delivery	Financial Services
Number of Employees	80,000	1,500	3,000	30,000	75	4,000	2,500
Age of Company	50	15	70	60	4	10	8
Employees Within IT	400	125	200	2,000	25	300	150
Processors Mainframe	4	0	0	8	0	2	0
Midrange	4	0	2	10	0	2	0
Servers	4	40	50	20	10	30	200
Desktops	1,200	600	2,000	5,000	80	1,800	1,500
# of Prod Apps	350	125	150	500	25	700	250
Apps Deployed/ Mo	2	2	3	4	1	3	5
Prod Svcs Dept	Yes	No	No	Yes	No	Yes	No
Dept To Which PS Reported	Ops	N/A	N/A	Ops	N/A	Apps Support	N/A
Quality Assurance Dept	No	No	Yes	Yes	No	Yes	No
Dept To Which QA Reported	N/A	N/A	Enterprise Planning	Apps Dev	N/A	Apps Dev	Apps Dev
Change Mgmt Formality	Medium	Low	Medium	High	None	Low	None
Prduction Acceptance Formality	Medium	None	Low	High	None	None	None

Figure 6–1 Summary comparison of case studies.

Another observation is that, with the exception of Company C, the older the company is, the more likely it is to have a PS group. This is further evidence that as client-server and Web-enabled environments become more prevalent, the less likely they are to embrace the PS function. This can eventually result in poorly deployed applications and unstable production environments that later require the benefits of a PS department.

We will next look at each of the seven companies in more detail, focusing on their use, or non-use, of a PS function. We will also discuss each IT organization's relative strengths and weaknesses, and what they learned from their experiences with attempting to implement robust infrastructure processes.

Company A

Company A is a large, well-established aerospace firm. The company is over 50 years old and enjoys a reputation for researching, developing, and applying cutting-edge technology for both the military and commercial sectors. At the time of our assignment, it employed 80,000 workers, of whom 400 resided in IT departments. The IT platform environment of its main corporate computer center consisted primarily of four huge mainframes, with the same number of midrange computers and servers and approximately 1,200 desktops.

The IT Operations department of Company A had a well-established PS function that ran 350 production applications daily, slightly more during month-end processing, and deployed an average of two new production applications per month. There was no QA group at this company, although they did have the beginnings of a formal Change Management and Production Acceptance process.

Two very competent individuals staffed the PS department who thoroughly knew the ins and outs of running virtually every production application in the company, although little of it was documented. They were very technically knowledgeable as was most all of the staff in IT. This reflected part of the company's mission to develop highly technical expertise throughout the enterprise. Another part of the company's mission was to dedicate every department to continuous process improvement. The PS function was still very manually oriented and consequently somewhat inefficient. No automated scheduling systems were in place at the time, but the company was willing to try new techniques and technologies to improve their processes.

Production Services was also very segregated from other processes such as Change and Problem Management. There was only the start of a Production Acceptance process, which was not tied to the PS function at all. This segregation occasionally strained communications between Operations and Applications Development. The fact that they were twenty-five miles apart sometimes added to the lack of effective face-to-face meetings.

Operations did a good job of collecting meaningful metrics such as outages, abnormal terminations, reruns, reprints, and reports delivered on time. There was an inconsistent emphasis on how often or how deeply their metrics should be analyzed, which sometimes undermined the usefulness of those metrics.

To summarize Company A's strengths, IT infrastructure managers were willing to try new techniques and new technologies, commit to continuous process improvement, hire and develop a technically competent staff, and were willing to collect meaningful metrics. To summarize their weaknesses, the managers tended to not interact with members of other IT staffs, provide little documented training, did not always have effective communications with the development group (due in part to a 25 mile separation), and did not always analyze the metrics they collected.

Eventually, the Operations department implemented a more formal Production Acceptance process. One of the most important lessons we learned was to ensure that the Operations department was involved very early with a new application project. This helps ensure that the appropriate Operations group provided or received the proper resources, capacity, documentation, and training required for a successful deployment. The other important lesson we learned was that the other Infrastructure Support groups such as Network Services, the Help Desk, Storage Management, and Desktop Services need to provide their full support to the PS function. Because this function had worked in an isolated manner in the past, other Infrastructure Support groups were initially reluctant to support it. With improved processes, automation, and increased communication, the problem of lack of support was resolved.

As mentioned in the previous chapter, many clients have asked me for a quick and simple method to evaluate the quality, efficiency, and effectiveness of their Production Acceptance processes. In response to these requests, we developed the Production Acceptance assessment worksheet shown in Figure 6–2. For Company A, the totals are 0 + 3 + 4 + 3 = 10. This total is then divided by the maximum possible rating of 30 for an assessment score of 33 percent. Keep in mind that we conducted the Production Acceptance process assessments prior to implementing any process improvements, and expected the scores to be in this range.

Apart from its obvious value of quantifying areas of strength and weakness for a given process, this rating provides two other significant benefits to an infrastructure. One is that it serves as a baseline benchmark from which future process refinements can be quantitatively measured and compared. The second is that the score of this particular process can be compared to those of other infrastructure processes to determine which ones need the most attention.

Company B

Company B is a satellite broadcast venture featuring informational programming. It is a relatively young firm—15 years old. When it began, the technology of digital informational broadcasting was in its early refinement stages. This, among other reasons, resulted in them being very willing to employ cutting-edge technology. They did this almost to a fault, using very advanced but questionably tested technology at the outset for their satellites. They learned from their experiences, improved their technology, and eventually applied what they had learned to their IT department by implementing cutting-edge, but proven, infrastructure processes.

Company B employed 1,500 workers, of whom 125 resided in IT. Their IT platform environment consists of 40 servers and approximately 600 desktops. There was no PS function at Company B, nor was there a QA group. They ran 125 production applications daily and deployed an average of two new production applications per month. There was only the beginning of a Change Management process and no Production Acceptance process at all.

With the company poised to implement major enterprise applications, senior IT management realized they needed a formal Production

Production Acceptance Process—Assessment Worksheet					
Process Owner__ Employee A__ Owner's Manager__ Manager A__ Date_N/A__					
Category	Questions for Production Acceptance	None	Small	Med	Lg
Executive Support	To what degree does the executive sponsor show support for the Production Acceptance process with actions such as engaging development managers and their staffs in this process?			2	
Process Owner	To what degree does the process owner exhibit desirable traits and understand Applications Development and deployment?				3
Customer Involvement	To what degree are key customers—especially from Development, Operations, and the Help Desk—involved in the design and use of the process?		1		
Supplier Involvement	To what degree are key suppliers, such as third-party vendors, trainers, and technical writers, involved in the design of the process?			2	
Service Metrics	To what degree are service metrics analyzed for trends, such as the amount of positive feedback from users and the number of calls to the Help Desk immediately after deployment?		1		
Process Metrics	To what degree are process metrics analyzed for trends such as the frequency and duration of delays to deployment and the accuracy and timelines of documentation and training?	0			
Process Integration	To what degree is the Production Acceptance process integrated with other processes and tools such as Change Management and Problem Management?	0			
Streamlining Automation	To what degree is the Production Acceptance process streamlined by automating actions such as the documentation of a new application and online training for it by means of the intranet?	0			
Training of Staff	To what degree is the staff cross-trained on the Production Acceptance process, and how is the effectiveness of the training verified?	0			
Process Documentation	To what degree is the quality and value of Production Acceptance documentation measured and maintained?		1		
	Totals	0	3	4	3
	Grand Total = 10				
Assessment Score = 10/33 = 33%					

Figure 6–2 Assessment worksheet for company A.

Acceptance process. While preferring to do the work with their own staff, they acknowledged their limited in-house process expertise and hired professional consultants to do a pilot program. The IT executives were also very helpful in supplying qualified staff members from both Applications Development and Operations to support the pilot program.

Because this was the first formal implementation of any infrastructure process, there was no integration to other processes and no immediate plans to do so. While Applications Development was extremely helpful in designing the Production Acceptance process and testing it with a perfect pilot application, they did not provide adequate training and documentation to the Operations Help Desk. This was partly due to a reshuffling of applications priorities that also delayed the implementation of the process with a fully deployed application.

To summarize Company B's strengths, the company saw the need for professional support for designing a Production Acceptance processes, started out with pilot programs, and staffed the pilot programs with qualified staff. Its weaknesses were that the company did not provide adequate training and documentation to the Help Desk group for their pilot program, it allowed support for the Production Acceptance process to weaken after the pilot program, and it did not formulate plans to integrate Production Acceptance with other processes.

The pilot program selected to test Company B's new Production Acceptance process was successfully deployed and proved the effectiveness of the process. Aside from the issue of Help Desk training and documentation, the most important lesson learned was the critical nature of ongoing executive support. As is the case with most infrastructure processes, external factors such as changing priorities, budget cuts, reorganizations, or management changes can quickly diminish the support of a new process. One of the best ways to prevent this is to have senior executives commit to the long-term support of a process prior to its design.

In a manner similar to that described for Company A, we performed an initial assessment of the Production Acceptance environment for Company B, as shown in Figure 6–3. The total points came to 8 for a final assessment score of 27 percent. This score was not surprising considering they had very little in the way of a Production Acceptance process at the time of the assessment.

Production Acceptance Process—Assessment Worksheet						
Process Owner __ Employee B __ Owner's Manager __ Manager B __ Date_N/A __						
Category	Questions for Production Acceptance	None	Small	Med	Lg
Executive Support	To what degree does the executive sponsor show support for the Production Acceptance process with actions such as engaging development managers and their staffs in this process?			2	
Process Owner	To what degree does the process owner exhibit desirable traits and understand Applications Development and deployment?			2	
Customer Involvement	To what degree are key customers—especially from Development, Operations, and the Help Desk—involved in the design and use of the process?		1		
Supplier Involvement	To what degree are key suppliers, such as third-party vendors, trainers, and technical writers, involved in the design of the process?		1		
Service Metrics	To what degree are service metrics analyzed for trends, such as the amount of positive feedback from users and the number of calls to the Help Desk immediately after deployment?	0			
Process Metrics	To what degree are process metrics analyzed for trends such as the frequency and duration of delays to deployment and the accuracy and timelines of documentation and training?	0			
Process Integration	To what degree is the Production Acceptance process integrated with other processes and tools such as Change Management and Problem Management?	0			
Streamlining Automation	To what degree is the Production Acceptance process streamlined by automating actions such as the documentation of a new application and online training for it by means of the intranet?	0			
Training of Staff	To what degree is the staff cross-trained on the Production Acceptance process, and how is the effectiveness of the training verified?		1		
Process Documentation	To what degree is the quality and value of Production Acceptance documentation measured and maintained?		1		
	Totals	0	4	4	0
	Grand Total = 8				
Assessment Score = 8/30 = 27%					

Figure 6–3 Assessment worksheet for company B.

Company C

Our third company is one of the seven major motion picture studios in southern California and is over 70 years old. Studios in Hollywood tend to be an interesting paradox. On one hand, they are some of the most creative companies for which one could ever hope to work. This applies to the writing, directing, acting, special effects, and other artistic pursuits that go into the production of a major motion picture. When it comes to the traditional, administrative support of the company, however, they are uncharacteristically conservative. This was especially true in their IT departments, and Company C was no different in this regard. By the late 1990s, its IT department needed to be significantly upgraded to meet aggressive new business expansions.

Company C employed 3,000 workers, of whom 200 resided in IT. Their IT platform environment consisted of two key midrange computers, 50 servers and approximately 2,000 desktops. The company outsourced its mainframe processing, which still runs many of its core financial systems. There was no PS function at Company C, but there was a QA department that reported to an enterprise-planning group. Operations ran 150 production applications daily and deployed an average of three new production applications per month. There was a formal, though not robust, Change Management process and an informal Production Acceptance process.

The IT executives at Company C conducted a studio-wide business assessment and determined that its current IT architecture would not support the future growth of the company. Many of the IT business systems would have to be upgraded or replaced, and there would have to be a major overhaul of the IT infrastructure and its processes to support the new application environment. Among the processes needing improving was Production Acceptance. IT managers recognized the need and the opportunity to reengineer their SDLC methodology at the same time, and committed the resources to do so. Software suppliers played key roles in these upgrades and reengineering efforts. Managers also ensured that users, both internal and external to IT, received sufficient training on these new processes.

The IT QA group at Company C worked closely with Operations and developers in chartering a PS function and in designing a Production Acceptance process. Because QA reported to the Applications Development department, IT executives elected to have the PS function report to them as well. This proved to be problematic in that the infrastructure group was often excluded from key deployment decisions. Another result of this arrangement was that it provided little documentation or training to the Help Desk and Computer Operations teams.

To sum up Company C's strengths, it recognized the need to upgrade its antiquated processes, it committed resources to reengineering the SDLC process, and it provided considerable training to users on new processes. As for its weaknesses, it did not involve the infrastructure when designing the Production Acceptance process, it moved the control of Production Acceptance into Applications Development and out of Operations, and it provided little or no training and documentation for the Help Desk and Operations.

Eventually, the PS function became little more than an extension of the QA department, which still reported to Applications Development. As a result, although the company did now have a Production Acceptance process in place, the lack of infrastructure ownership of it made it less robust and effective. The key lesson learned here was that IT executives must ensure that Operations controls the Production Acceptance process, and that development be involved in the process design from the start.

In a similar manner to that described for Company A, we performed an initial assessment of the Production Acceptance process for Company C, as shown in Figure 6–4. Their points totalled 9 for a final assessment score of 30 percent.

Company D

This company was a major defense contractor who supplied major weapons systems to the United States and foreign governments for over sixty years. Its customers were primarily the five branches of the United States armed forces, as well as (secondarily) the militaries of foreign governments. The company managed both classified and nonclassified programs, putting an additional premium on fail-safe security systems. It also supplied limited commercial aviation products.

At the time of our involvement, Company D employed 30,000 workers, of whom 2,000 resided in IT. Their IT platform environment consisted of eight mainframes, 10 midrange computers, 20 servers and 5,000 desktops. There was a relatively formal PS function at Company D that reported to Operations, and a QA group that reported to Applications

Category	Questions for Production Acceptance	None	Small	Med	Lg
	Production Acceptance Process—Assessment Worksheet				
	Process Owner __ Employee C __ Owner's Manager __ Manager C __ Date_N/A __				
Executive Support	To what degree does the executive sponsor show support for the Production Acceptance process with actions such as engaging development managers and their staffs in this process?		1		
Process Owner	To what degree does the process owner exhibit desirable traits and understand Applications Development and deployment?		1		
Customer Involvement	To what degree are key customers—especially from Development, Operations, and the Help Desk—involved in the design and use of the process?		1		
Supplier Involvement	To what degree are key suppliers, such as third-party vendors, trainers, and technical writers, involved in the design of the process?			2	
Service Metrics	To what degree are service metrics analyzed for trends, such as the amount of positive feedback from users and the number of calls to the Help Desk immediately after deployment?	0			
Process Metrics	To what degree are process metrics analyzed for trends such as the frequency and duration of delays to deployment and the accuracy and timelines of documentation and training?	0			
Process Integration	To what degree is the Production Acceptance process integrated with other processes and tools such as Change Management and Problem Management?	0			
Streamlining Automation	To what degree is the Production Acceptance process streamlined by automating actions such as the documentation of a new application and online training for it by means of the intranet?		1		
Training of Staff	To what degree is the staff cross-trained on the Production Acceptance process, and how is the effectiveness of the training verified?			2	
Process Documentation	To what degree is the quality and value of Production Acceptance documentation measured and maintained?		1		
	Totals	0	5	4	0
	Grand Total = 9				
Assessment Score = 9/30 = 30%					

Figure 6–4   Assessment worksheet for company C.

Development. They ran 500 production applications daily, dozens more on weekends, and deployed on average four new production applications per month. The company had very formal Change Management and Production Acceptance processes, and was very committed to the practices of total quality and continuous process improvement.

The company also emphasized the use and analysis of meaningful metrics. By meaningful, we mean metrics that our customers and we, as suppliers, can both use to improve the level of our services. One of the most refreshing aspects of this company was their support of our prescribed process improvement sequence of integrating first, standardizing second, streamlining third, and automating last.

As with many government defense contractors, Company D found itself rushing to meet program milestones, and this sometimes undermined infrastructure processes such as Production Acceptance. High priority projects were allowed to bypass the process to meet critical deadlines. Plans to streamline and automate the Production Acceptance process became a victim of unfortunate timing. Just as they were about to be put into place, cutbacks in personnel prevented the plans from being implemented. Subsequent mergers and acquisitions brought about some temporary turf wars that further delayed the standardization of processes across all divisions.

To summarize Company D's strengths, there was a *commitment* to total quality and continuous process improvement criteria, doing excellent analysis of metrics, and striving to sequentially integrate, standardize, streamline, and then automate processes. To summarize the weaknesses, Company D was undermining the Production Acceptance process by rushing to meet deadlines, allowing high priority projects to bypass the process, not allowing the process to be streamlined due to cutbacks, and experiencing occasional turf wars between IT departments.

Eventually, the standardization, streamlining, and automating of processes did occur among departments and across divisions and remote sites, and brought with it significant operation and financial benefits. The standardization also helped facilitate future company acquisitions and the merging of remote sites.

As we did with our prior companies, we performed an initial assessment of the Production Acceptance environment for Company D, as shown in Figure 6–5. They scored one of the highest initial assessments we had ever seen. Their total points came to 21 for a final assessment score of 70 percent.

Production Acceptance Process—Assessment Worksheet					
Process Owner __ Employee D __ Owner's Manager __ Manager D __ Date_N/A __					
Category	Questions for Production Acceptance	None	Small	Med	Lg
Executive Support	To what degree does the executive sponsor show support for the Production Acceptance process with actions such as engaging development managers and their staffs in this process?			2	
Process Owner	To what degree does the process owner exhibit desirable traits and understand Applications Development and deployment?				3
Customer Involvement	To what degree are key customers—especially from Development, Operations, and the Help Desk— involved in the design and use of the process?				3
Supplier Involvement	To what degree are key suppliers, such as third-party vendors, trainers, and technical writers, involved in the design of the process?			2	
Service Metrics	To what degree are service metrics analyzed for trends, such as the amount of positive feedback from users and the number of calls to the Help Desk immediately after deployment?			2	
Process Metrics	To what degree are process metrics analyzed for trends such as the frequency and duration of delays to deployment and the accuracy and timelines of documentation and training?			2	
Process Integration	To what degree is the Production Acceptance process integrated with other processes and tools such as Change Management and Problem Management?		1		
Streamlining Automation	To what degree is the Production Acceptance process streamlined by automating actions such as the documentation of a new application and online training for it by means of the intranet?				3
Training of Staff	To what degree is the staff cross-trained on the Production Acceptance process, and how is the effectiveness of the training verified?				3
Process Documentation	To what degree is the quality and value of Production Acceptance documentation measured and maintained?			2	
	Totals	0	1	8	12
	Grand Total = 21				
Assessment Score = 21/30 = 70%					

Figure 6–5 Assessment worksheet for company D.

Company E

Our next company was a dotcom victim, but fortunately not a casualty. Like many dotcom start-ups that came before it, this company began with a simple idea. Company E wanted to offer pop culture merchandise from television, motion pictures, sports, and other forms of entertainment. It had been in existence barely four years, and was poised for significant growth. A shrinking national economy, coupled with fierce competition on the Internet, forced dramatic cutbacks in the company. It did survive, but on a much smaller scale.

Company E employed 75 workers, 25 of whom resided in IT departments. Their IT platform environment consisted of 10 servers and 80 desktops. There was no PS function at Company E, nor was there a QA group. They ran 25 production applications daily and deployed an average of one new production application per month. The initial priorities of the company were to get their Website up and operational, and to start producing revenue. As a result, there was no Change Management or Production Acceptance processes in place. As the company started to grow, the need for these processes became more apparent.

Since the company was starting with a clean slate, there were no previous processes to undo, replace, or reengineer. There were many young, energetic individuals at Company E who were eager to learn new skills and methods. The relatively small profile of applications meant that we had a large number from which to select a pilot program. A willing staff and a select group of pilot applications could not overcome the problems and changing priorities of the company's rapid growth. Just as a process was about to be implemented, a new crisis would arise that put the new procedure on hold.

A larger challenge common to many dotcom companies was the culture clashes that arose between the entrepreneurial spirit of those behind the company's initial success and the more disciplined approach of those charged with implementing structured processes into the environment. The clash was especially evident between the technical gurus who were used to having free reign when deploying new applications, installing upgrades, or making routine maintenance changes. Those of us tasked with implementing infrastructure processes spent a fair amount of time negotiating, compromising, and marketing before achieving some positive results.

To summarize Company E's strengths, it was a high-energy start-up with no prior processes needing to be reengineered, it had only a small profile of existing applications with many new ones planned that allowed for a number of pilot programs, and it enjoyed a young staff eager to learn new methods. Its weaknesses included its rapid growth, which hindered the use of processes, its entrepreneurial culture that clashed with disciplined processes, and its influential technical gurus who were, at times, unwilling to support new processes.

Despite these drawbacks, we were able to design and pilot an initial Production Acceptance process. The process was much more streamlined than normal due to the accelerated nature of Web-enabled applications. This streamlining actually helped to integrate it with a pilot Change Management process that was also being developed. The frequency of new application builds in this Internet environment made Change Management and Production Acceptance almost indistinguishable at times. This integration also facilitated much cross training between infrastructure groups and Applications Development to ensure both areas understood the others as changes and deployments were being planned.

As we did with our prior companies, we performed an initial assessment of the Production Acceptance environment for Company E, as shown in Figure 6–6. As you might expect with a start-up, the assessment was relatively low, although they did score well for process integration and cross training. Their total points came to 8 for a final assessment score of 27 percent.

Company F

This company did everything right—almost. It broke off from a relatively rigid, conservative parent company and vowed to be more flexible, progressive, and streamlined. The IT executives understood the importance of robust infrastructure processes and committed the resources to make them a reality. Their only flaw was diving headfirst into Production Acceptance before any semblance of a Change Management process was put in place.

Company F employed 4,000 workers, of whom 300 resided in IT departments. Their IT platform environment consisted of two mainframe processors, two midrange computers, 30 servers and approximately 1,800

Production Acceptance Process—Assessment Worksheet					
Process Owner __ Employee E __ Owner's Manager __ Manager E __ Date_N/A __					
Category	Questions for Production Acceptance	None	Small	Med	Lg
Executive Support	To what degree does the executive sponsor show support for the Production Acceptance process with actions such as engaging development managers and their staffs in this process?		1		
Process Owner	To what degree does the process owner exhibit desirable traits and understand Applications Development and deployment?	0			
Customer Involvement	To what degree are key customers—especially from Development, Operations, and the Help Desk— involved in the design and use of the process?		1		
Supplier Involvement	To what degree are key suppliers, such as third-party vendors, trainers, and technical writers, involved in the design of the process?		1		
Service Metrics	To what degree are service metrics analyzed for trends, such as the amount of positive feedback from users and the number of calls to the Help Desk immediately after deployment?	0			
Process Metrics	To what degree are process metrics analyzed for trends such as the frequency and duration of delays to deployment and the accuracy and timelines of documentation and training?	0			
Process Integration	To what degree is the Production Acceptance process integrated with other processes and tools such as Change Management and Problem Management?			2	
Streamlining Automation	To what degree is the Production Acceptance process streamlined by automating actions such as the documentation of a new application and online training for it by means of the intranet?		1		
Training of Staff	To what degree is the staff cross-trained on the Production Acceptance process, and how is the effectiveness of the training verified?			2	
Process Documentation	To what degree is the quality and value of Production Acceptance documentation measured and maintained?	0			
	Totals	0	4	4	0
	Grand Total = 8				
Assessment Score = 8/30 = 27%					

Figure 6–6   Assessment worksheet for company E.

desktops. There was a PS department at Company F that reported to an Applications Support group, and there was a QA group that reported to Applications Development. They ran 700 production applications daily, a dozen or so more on weekends and during month-end closings, and deployed an average of three new production applications per month. There was only the start of a Change Management process and no Production Acceptance process.

When the company first asked us to upgrade their IT environment by implementing robust infrastructure processes, they suggested we begin with Production Acceptance. They reasoned that since they were planning to deploy several new critical applications during the upcoming year, and already had an Applications Support group in place, that this would be the natural place to start. We conducted an initial assessment of their infrastructure and concluded that a Change Management process was more urgently needed than Production Acceptance. We based this conclusion on the number and variety of changes being made to their production environment locally and remotely, and that both were increasing at an accelerated rate.

The IT executives were very receptive to our recommendation about Change Management and were very supportive of our efforts to involve various departments within IT. They suggested that we include the remote sites as part of our strategy and committed time and resources to the process. Including the remote sites was a key addition because it allowed us to standardize and integrate the process across all locations. Even though a partial Change Management process was already in place, the IT managers realized its disjointed nature and its lack of metrics, and were willing to design a new process from scratch. In the past they were not aware of the importance of collecting or analyzing metrics; eventually they were won over after seeing how effective they could be in managing changes and new deployments.

One downside during our involvement at Company F was the frequent reorganizations, especially concerning Operations, Applications Support, and our new PS function. This delayed some of the process approvals and made some of the managers unwilling to select a pilot project for Production Acceptance because responsibilities for certain applications were likely to change.

As for Company F's strengths, the company recognized that Change Management needed to be implemented prior to any other infrastructure processes, its IT executives provided strong support for these processes, it included its remote sites as part of the strategy, and it was willing to start with a clean slate. As for its weaknesses, Company F saw little need for the use of metrics, exhibited no recognition of the need to analyze metrics, implemented frequent reorganizations that undermined attempts at process improvements, and showed an unwillingness to nominate a pilot Production Acceptance project.

Despite these hurdles, a very effective Change Management process was implanted at Company F. There was total standardization among three sites separated by over a thousand miles. There were service and process metrics in place that were regularly collected, analyzed, and distributed. It laid the foundation for a Production Acceptance process that would shortly follow. The most significant lesson learned was how important it was to implement key processes in the proper sequence. We would not have been as successful with either Change Management or Production Acceptance if we had not implemented them in the order we did.

As we did with our prior companies, we performed an initial assessment of the Production Acceptance environment for Company F, as shown in Figure 6–7. Their prior establishment of an Applications Support group resulted in having good service metrics that were collected and analyzed on a regular basis. Their total points came to 19 for a final assessment score of 63 percent.

Company G

Company G was a relatively young financial services establishment that began eight years ago. It was successfully transitioning from a small start-up to a medium-sized enterprise. We have seen many a company at a similar time in their development struggle to transform from a novice firm into a mature organization. Company G did not seem to be struggling in this transformation. They have effectively promoted a culture of empowerment, honesty, and change, and it is very much in evidence in their everyday manner of doing business.

Company G employed 2,500 workers, of whom 150 reside in IT departments. Their IT platform environment consists of 200 servers and approximately 1,500 desktops. The reason they have such a large number of servers in relation to desktops is that for several years each new

Category	Questions for Production Acceptance	None	Small	Med	Lg
Executive Support	To what degree does the executive sponsor show support for the Production Acceptance process with actions such as engaging development managers and their staffs in this process?			2	
Process Owner	To what degree does the process owner exhibit desirable traits and understand Applications Development and deployment?			2	
Customer Involvement	To what degree are key customers—especially from Development, Operations, and the Help Desk— involved in the design and use of the process?			2	
Supplier Involvement	To what degree are key suppliers, such as third-party vendors, trainers, and technical writers, involved in the design of the process?			2	
Service Metrics	To what degree are service metrics analyzed for trends, such as the amount of positive feedback from users and the number of calls to the Help Desk immediately after deployment?				3
Process Metrics	To what degree are process metrics analyzed for trends such as the frequency and duration of delays to deployment and the accuracy and timelines of documentation and training?			2	
Process Integration	To what degree is the Production Acceptance process integrated with other processes and tools such as Change Management and Problem Management?		1		
Streamlining Automation	To what degree is the Production Acceptance process streamlined by automating actions such as the documentation of a new application and online training for it by means of the intranet?		1		
Training of Staff	To what degree is the staff cross-trained on the Production Acceptance process, and how is the effectiveness of the training verified?			2	
Process Documentation	To what degree is the quality and value of Production Acceptance documentation measured and maintained?	3			
	Totals	0	2	14	3
	Grand Total = 19				
Assessment Score = 19/30 = 63%					

Production Acceptance Process—Assessment Worksheet

Process Owner __ Employee F __ Owner's Manager __ Manager F __ Date_N/A __

Figure 6–7 Assessment worksheet for company F.

application was given its own server. This was one of several reasons for instituting a Production Acceptance process. There was no PS function at Company G, although there was a QA group that reported to Applications Development. They ran 250 production applications daily and deployed an average of five new production applications per month. There was only the start of a Change Management process and no Production Acceptance process at the time we initiated our involvement.

Because the company was so young, it had few infrastructure processes in place. The up side to this was that there were few poor processes that would need to be reworked. IT executives recognized the need to implement robust infrastructure processes, and were willing to hire full-time staff to help implement and maintain them—particularly Change Management, Production Acceptance, and business continuity. They also saw the huge benefits to be gained from integrating these processes and stressed the need to design and implement these processes in a coordinated fashion.

The company did have a few hurdles to overcome. Audits are a fact of life in the banking and financial services industry, and Company G had their share of them. This sometimes caused them to focus more on the results of audits than on the quality of their processes and services. Another hurdle was the lack of experience of critical team leads. This was not the fault of the leads. The company believed strongly in promoting from within, and with such a young organization this meant the leads needed some time to grow into their jobs. The company invested well in training and mentoring to address this.

The rapid growth of the company also caused many shifts in priorities. This caused some pilot applications for Production Acceptance to change, causing the pilot to be restarted more than once. The Production Acceptance process did integrate well into their SDLC methodology, although an exorbitant amount of detail went into the analyses of these processes. Their point total of 14 produced an assessment score of 47 percent, as shown in Figure 6–8.

In review of Company G's strengths, it provided a highly empowering environment, it was a relatively young firm with few poor processes, it integrated their processes well, and it was willing to hire full-time staff to implement a Production Acceptance process. As for its weaknesses, staff sometimes placed more emphasis on audits than on results, the company had a lack of experienced team leads, its rapid growth caused

Production Acceptance Process—Assessment Worksheet					
Process Owner __ Employee G __ Owner's Manager __ Manager G __ Date_N/A __					
Category	Questions for Production Acceptance	None	Small	Med	Lg
Executive Support	To what degree does the executive sponsor show support for the Production Acceptance process with actions such as engaging development managers and their staffs in this process?		1		
Process Owner	To what degree does the process owner exhibit desirable traits and understand Applications Development and deployment?		1		
Customer Involvement	To what degree are key customers—especially from Development, Operations, and the Help Desk—involved in the design and use of the process?		1		
Supplier Involvement	To what degree are key suppliers, such as third-party vendors, trainers, and technical writers, involved in the design of the process?			2	
Service Metrics	To what degree are service metrics analyzed for trends, such as the amount of positive feedback from users and the number of calls to the Help Desk immediately after deployment?		1		
Process Metrics	To what degree are process metrics analyzed for trends such as the frequency and duration of delays to deployment and the accuracy and timelines of documentation and training?	0			
Process Integration	To what degree is the Production Acceptance process integrated with other processes and tools such as Change Management and Problem Management?				3
Streamlining Automation	To what degree is the Production Acceptance process streamlined by automating actions such as the documentation of a new application and online training for it by means of the intranet?		1		
Training of Staff	To what degree is the staff cross-trained on the Production Acceptance process, and how is the effectiveness of the training verified?			2	
Process Documentation	To what degree is the quality and value of Production Acceptance documentation measured and maintained?			2	
	Totals	0	5	6	3
	Grand Total = 14				
Assessment Score = 14/30 = 47%					

Figure 6–8 Assessment worksheet for company G.

frequent priority changes, and its Production Acceptance analysis is overly detailed.

This company used three excellent strategies in its process improvement efforts. The first was to use a simple design in its processes, the second was to use widely accepted tools, and the third was to have wide-spread involvement and agreement by multiple groups to ensure the required *buy-in* from all required areas. These strategies worked very well in fashioning processes that were efficient, effective, and widely used.

This concludes our discussion of our process experiences at seven client companies. Figure 6–9 presents a summary comparison of each company's relative strengths and weaknesses, as well as the lessons we and they learned from our process improvement efforts.

Summary

This chapter presented our experiences at seven different companies involving infrastructure processes in general, and the Production Acceptance process in particular. The companies offered a wide variety of industries, size, age, platforms, and cultures. As such, each afforded us a unique opportunity to identify their weaknesses, build on their strengths, and learn from the many lessons they experienced. Each company's experiences were described at some length. Finally, we presented a summary comparison of each company's business and technical profiles, along with their relative strengths, weaknesses, and the lessons learned from our efforts to improve their processes.

	Company A	Company B	Company C	Company D	Company E	Company F	Company G
S **T** **R** **E** **N** **G** **T** **H** **S**	• willing to try new techniques • committed to continuous process improvement • technically competent staff • willing to collect meaningful metrics	• saw need for professional support for designing PA processes • started out with pilot programs • staffed pilot programs with qualified staff	• recognized need to upgrade processes • included good use of suppliers • committed resources to re-engineer SDLC • provided much training to users	• committed to Baldridge quality award criteria • analyzed metrics well • strives to integrate, standardize, streamline, and then automate	• high energy start-up with no prior processes to reengineer • small profile of applications allowed for many pilots • young staff eager to learn	• recognized that Change Management must come first • total support of IT executives • remote sites part of strategy • willing to start with clean slate	• highly empowering environment • few poor processes • much process integration • willing to hire full-time staff to implement PA

Figure 6–9 Comparative strengths and weaknesses of seven companies.

	Company A	Company B	Company C	Company D	Company E	Company F	Company G
W E A K N E S S E S	• tend to not interact with staff • little documented training • Operations and Development groups physically apart by 25 miles • collected metrics, but did not always analyze them	• did not provide training and documentation to Help Desk group • support for PA process weakened after pilot program • no plans to integrate with other processes	• did not involve the infrastruture • moved the control of PA into Development out of Operations • little or no training and documentation for Help Desk and Operations	• rush to meet deadlines undermines following the PA process • high priority projects allowed to bypass process • process not streamlined due to cutbacks • turf wars	• rapid growth hindered use of processes • entrepreneurial culture clashed with disciplined processses • influential gurus unwilling to support new processes	• saw little need of use of metrics • no recognition of need to analyze metrics	• more emphasis on audits than on results • lack of experienced team leads • rapid growth caused frequent priority changes • PA analysis overly detailed
L E S S O N S	• Development and Operations need to work together from the start • Infrastructure Services Organizations need to support the PA process and operations	• ensure the long-range commitments of IT • consider a Change Management process prior to a PA process	• IT executives must ensure that Operations controls the PA process, and that Development be inviolved in the process design from the start	• there are significant benefits from standardizing across all divisions and remote sites, and this helps merger integration	• one needs to be aware of changing and conflicting cultures due to the unstructured and entreprenuerial nature of startups	• important to implement key processes in proper sequence such as a Change Management process prior to Production Services	• use simple, widely agreed upon processes, strategies and tools in order to ensure the buy-in of all required support groups

Figure 6–9 Comparative strengths and weaknesses of seven companies. (Continued)

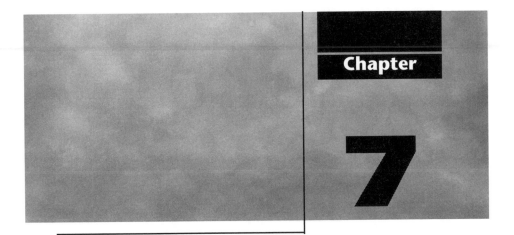

Most Frequently Asked Questions

Introduction

This chapter presents some of the most frequently asked questions (and our responses to them) that we receive while conducting workshops, assessing infrastructures, and consulting with leading IT organizations around the world. The questions cover a wide variety of IT topics, with many of them centering around the issues of infrastructure organizations, people, and processes.

Q1. The Production Control organization died with the mainframe world; why are you trying to bring it back to life?

A1. The Production Control organization was once commonly referred to as the production gatekeepers. They held the key to Reliability, Availability, and Serviceability (RAS). Without the Production Control group, there would be no assurance of RAS in the legacy world or with client-server computing. Their crowning responsibility was to provide

24×7 availability for all mission-critical systems. Their charter evolved around RAS.

The Production Control group's main functions were as follows:

- Providing 2nd level production support
- Assisting senior technical staff in the analysis, implementation, and customization of enterprise-wide system management tools
- Assisting senior technical staff in providing junior Systems Administration functions O/S support, hardware setup, on-call support, etc.
- Processing ownership (Production Acceptance, Change Control, etc.)
- Breeding ground for technical resources

The lack of a Production Control function in the 21st century has raised issues such as:

- Ineffective or missing enterprise-wide processes
- System management tools not fully implemented
- Technical staff in constant reactive mode
- Lack of technical resources
- Difficulties retaining senior technical resources

We are now introducing the new and improved Production Control function, which we refer to as *Production Services (PS)*. The old Production Control function was not customer service oriented—everything was one sided, dictated by the Production Control group. A key component of the PS function is Production Acceptance, which puts the customer(s) of the system first.

Q2. Why is it so important to have a production Quality Assurance (QA) function for the Infrastructure Services Organization?

A2. QA has been a critical function within IT for decades. In the legacy environment, it was much easier to control change (the pace of system or application deployment). All changes from the Applications Development side of IT went through a rigorous QA process. It wasn't very customer friendly, but it did the job. It was rare for a new release of an application or a brand new application to contaminate the sacred production environment.

The primary focus of today's QA function is version and release management of new code. This is still a critical function. The Production Services QA function focuses its efforts on aligning the production support staff with Applications Development to ensure that all operational requirements will be addressed before deploying that new system into production (see Chapter 5). It also clearly defines everyone's roles and responsibilities by application for ongoing production support.

With the advent of network computing, new applications or enhancements to existing systems are being developed and deployed in weeks versus the legacy world where it took months or years to develop and deploy new systems. These new systems were thrown over the wall from development to production without a thorough test process. The same production QA function that was so effective in the mainframe world was no longer adequate to keep up with the "Internet-speed" world of network computing. The need for a reengineered production QA process was here. We refer to this process as *Production Acceptance*.

Q3.   You discuss Production Acceptance as being the key constituent for promoting effective communication practices—how can a process promote effective communication practices?

A3.   Monthly or quarterly departmental meetings are not the answer. Communication needs to be practiced and exercised daily via a process. The essential benefit and the primary reason the Production Acceptance process was designed was to improve communications.

Throughout the application deployment phase, a person from (communication liaison) Production Services (PS) is assigned to work with the project leader of the new system or application. Once the PS person is enlisted he/she will engage other individuals from the Infrastructure Services Organization at appropriate intervals. The PS's primary responsibility is to bring key people from the business unit, Applications Development, and Infrastructure Support together via the Production Acceptance process.

Have we been successful? Without a doubt everywhere we have consulted on the implementation of this process it has improved communications throughout IT and external to IT.

Q4.   What type of individual would meet the job requirements for Production Services?

A4.   The best qualified individual has to have excellent people and process skills. Ideally it would be nice to promote from within or hire someone with a data center Operations background in a large shop that practices RAS. This individual would also need to have a good grasp of technology.

A primary responsibility for this individual is being able to market, sell, and obtain *buy-in* for key enterprise-wide processes. Because the group will own the Production Acceptance and Change Management processes, this individual needs to have good negotiating skills with all levels of IT. This type of individual is worth his weight in gold, and yes they are rare to find. See Appendix A for a description of a Director of Production Services and a Senior Process Engineer.

Q5. I work in a large heterogeneous IT organization, and it appears like the mainframe applications are turned over to production in an orderly yet very bureaucratic fashion. Applications Development on the other hand, continuously shoves the client-server systems down the throats of our Infrastructure Support staff, without a formal process. Is it possible to use the mainframe processes to manage our client-server environment?

A5. The mainframe processes are too bureaucratic and the client-server environment typically utilizes very few or no disciplines (processes). If you adhere to *Commandment #6* (see Chapter 2), then destiny is in your hands. You need a happy medium between too much discipline and not enough. In our book entitled *IT Organization* where we have done extensive studies on IT infrastructure, you need to focus on fully implementing only three to four processes. The key factors are to market and sell the process within your organization first and then sell it to your customers. If you cannot get 100 percent *buy-in* within IT infrastructures, then do not bother selling it to your customers—it is probably too bureaucratic.

Potential mainframe, data center customers had to fill out a document called a *runbook* before introducing their systems into production. The *runbook* was a process addressing the following requirements:

- Scheduling information

- Application description

- Who does the data center Operations staff call in the middle of the night when there are problems?

- Special scheduling dependencies

These requirements were sufficient for the closed architecture, bureaucratic, and not very customer-oriented legacy environment. In today's heterogeneous, global, and customer-wants-everything-yesterday attitude, however, these processes will not work.

Each process designed in the mainframe era needs to be re-engineered for simplicity to support a heterogeneous environment. Each process needs to be designed with the minimum/sufficient requirements in mind. First and foremost, IT needs to keep the customer in mind when designing the process.

If the process you are designing directly affects the customer, then you need to have them involved in any pilot (process rollout). *Buy-in* is the KEY to success with any process—never design a process in a vacuum or you will fail.

Below are some of the key attributes we designed into a new and improved *runbook*, which is now a part of our Production Acceptance process:

- Improve communications within IT and external to IT
- Develop SLAs with our customers
- Identify key participants roles and responsibilities for every mission-critical application
- Adherence to key Infrastructure Support standards

Q6.   Our organization is small and we have very few resources—how will the lack of a PS function affect us?

A6.   Although you have a small organization, a few critical processes are still a requirement. Some of the most critical processes (based on over a hundred assessments—see our book entitled *IT Organization*) are Problem Management, Change Management, and Production Acceptance. Obviously, security and business continuity have become priority as well ever since September 11th, 2001, but we're assuming these are already being addressed. These processes (if implemented and adhered to) will make your small organization much more efficient. Without these processes, it will be impossible to obtain and maintain RAS with limited resources.

Regardless of the size of your organization, implementing part or all of a PS function is a requirement.

Q7.   Why is the Production Control function from the legacy environment not sufficient for Network Computing?

A7.   One of the biggest reasons the mainframe environment became so unpopular with the user community was because processes were unilateral. The Production Control group never put the customer first. It didn't matter what the customer's requirements were. The group put

RAS first. The customer became an afterthought. No one had the time to properly communicate with the customer. The lack of communication between IT and their customers was why the QA function was so ineffective. The goal was to maintain Reliable, Available, Serviceable (RAS)—a full time effort.

With the advent of client-server, customers found freedom from corporate IT. They no longer had rules to follow. There were no corporate standards to follow, bureaucratic processes to adhere to, etc. In the mainframe days, it could take years to develop new systems; now that these customers were cranking out new systems in months or even weeks, each business unit wanted efficient and spontaneous service. They did not want to be put into a queue for service. They wanted to be treated with respect for the first time in the history of corporate computing.

The Production Acceptance process puts the customer first and focuses on three primary functions:

- Communication
- Communication
- Communication

Yes, we typed it three times to prove a point—the importance of over-communicating. There is no such thing as overcommunicating in IT.

Q8. What is RAS? Why is it so important?

A8. Reliable, Available, Serviceable (RAS) stood for computing excellence. It was the methodology to safeguard the company's mission-critical production systems. RAS is so much more than an acronym. In the 1970s and 1980s, it was a way of life for data processing professionals.

RAS stood for discipline. System management processes (i.e., Change Management) were processes that insured high availability. No one (absolutely no one) was allowed to tamper with the production environment without going through this stringent process. RAS was also documented procedures for all production support functions, practiced Disaster Recovery process, and data center Facilities Management.

While working in that glass house, we were instructed that everything inside those glass walls was sacred. Everything had a price tag associated with system downtime. We knew exactly what it would cost the company if any particular system were down for any length of time.

There was a reason those Management Information Systems (MIS) directors of yesteryear held unexpected data center inspections. You may have undoubtedly heard the stories about the executives putting on their white gloves while casually strolling through their resplendent glass house. They were looking in every nook and cranny—even lifting the removable tile (raised floor)—searching for dirt. Unreal, but true! Anything at all that could potentially cause downtime was not tolerated.

When we performed IT assessments of Global 2000 and Fortune 500 companies, we discovered that most of the problems and issues today had evolved from ignoring RAS.

Q9. Once an organization takes so much time and resources to design and develop a Production Acceptance process, how do you ensure success?

A9. One of the key success factors to any process is *buy-in*. Without *buy-in*, the process will fail. In the case of Production Acceptance, where it interfaces with every group in IT and many customers on the business side, *buy-in* is the top priority. To ensure *buy-in* across the organization, we recommend that you invest in an IT Planning and Development workshop (see Chapter 3).

If this is the initial implementation of Production Acceptance, you will also need to spend a good deal of time marketing and selling the product (see the books entitled *Building The New Enterprise* and *IT Services* on how to effectively market and sell your services within IT and external to IT). The best way to get *buy-in* is to involve as many of the following people as possible in a pilot project:

- Application developers
- Project leaders
- Business analysts/liaisons
- Systems Administrators
- Help Desk personnel
- Database Administrators
- Customers

Start with a non-mission-critical system. Once you are successful deploying the system into production and Reliable, Available, Serviceable (RAS) is attained, these customers will become supplementary resources in a short time to help market and sell the process to diverging groups. Other success factors are:

- Start early; do not wait until an application is nearly ready for production

- Intimately involve developers and users; build their sense of ownership. Let them feel like they own the process. Listen to their ideas. They need to feel empowered

- Always go through the Production Acceptance process for new applications and releases—no exceptions

- Clearly spell out and document everyone's roles and responsibilities

Q10. What are some of the risks of not having a Production Acceptance process?

A10. Some of the risks of not having a Production Acceptance process entail:

- Implementing an application into production without thorough testing and not having the proper documentation

- Treating every application as an exception and taking shortcuts

- Reassigning application developers to new projects before completing deployment of current application

- Procrastinating or being too preoccupied to thoroughly document

- Allowing the Production Acceptance process to gather dust—not making it an ongoing process

Q11. What are the benefits to implementing a Production Acceptance process?

A11. When an organization implements a Production Acceptance process the benefits are all-encompassing for all departments. For example:

To Applications:

- Ensures adequate network and system capacity is available for both development and production

- Identifies desktop upgrade requirements in advance to ensure sufficient budget, resources, and timeframe

- Specifies detailed hardware and software configurations of both the development and production servers to ensure identical environments are used for testing and deployment

- Ensures Infrastructure Support groups (systems, networks, solution center) are trained on supporting the application weeks prior to cutover

To Executive Management:

- Quantifies total ongoing support costs prior to project start-up
- Reduces overtime costs by identifying upgrade requirements early on
- Greater likelihood of meeting scheduled deployment by ensuring thorough and timely testing

To Infrastructure:

- Identifies initial system and network requirements early on
- Identifies future infrastructure requirements enabling more cost-effective Capacity Planning
- Identifies ongoing support requirements early on

To Customers:

- Involves customers early on in the planning phase
- Ensures customer equipment upgrades are identified early on and scheduled with customer involvement
- Ensures satisfactory user testing
- Improves communication between customers and IT

To Suppliers:

- Involves key suppliers in the success of the project
- Partners key suppliers with each other and with support groups
- Provides suppliers with opportunities to suggest improvements for deployment

Q12. What are the differences between Production Acceptance and Change Management?

A12. Production Acceptance is used for transitioning all new mission-critical systems or major existing system revisions into production. Production Acceptance is used to insure that infrastructure support requirements are addressed from system inception until it is migrated into production. We define systems as applications or system management tools that typically reside in a mission-critical production environment requiring 24×7 support.

Change Management is a process used to document and communicate all changes (network, OS, facilities, applications, etc.) that could impact the production environment.

Q13. We have limited resources and no money budgeted for process implementation; where do we begin?

A13. We have yet to see a single IT department budget resources for the implementation of infrastructure processes. Executives in the approval cycle typically cut these budget items without question. Customarily, predestined initiatives (i.e., training and process development) get slashed from the yearly IT budget planning process. You may have to develop a mini version of some of the most critical processes (i.e., Production Acceptance)—maybe just a checklist of requirements for Applications Development before they deploy the system into production. You have to do it in some way (i.e., on your own time).

Q14. When should an infrastructure organization first get involved with Production Acceptance?

A14. An infrastructure organization should first get involved with Production Acceptance as soon as a new application is approved for implementation. This will ensure that Operations personnel and capacity planners are involved up front.

Q15. Which infrastructure factors usually delay deployment of a new application?

A15. More times than not a new application is delayed by the infrastructure failing to provide adequate capacity of resources. These may be in the form of processing power of servers, amount of usable disk space, or even desktop capacities such as processor speed, memory size, or printer capability.

Q16. What is the best way for the Infrastructure Services Organization to prevent delays in deploying a new application due to lack of adequate capacities?

A16. Work with developers to create an accurate forecast of the capacity requirements of the new application well in advance of the launch date and ensure all requirements are identified and met in time.

Q17. What role, if any, does Desktop Services play in Production Acceptance?

A17. Desktop Services plays a very key role in Production Acceptance in that the proper quantity of, and upgrades to, appropriate desktops must be in place prior to the initial date of production.

Q18. What role, if any, does the Help Desk play in the Production Acceptance process?

A18. Help Desk personnel need to have the proper documentation and be trained to effectively support all new applications being transitioned from development to production.

Q19. What happens if a system has not fully completed the Production Acceptance process, yet due to political pressure the system is forced into production?

A19. Do *not* compromise by potentially contaminating your production environment with systems that are not thoroughly tested and documented. A happy medium is to establish a preproduction environment on a separate subnet with a minimal set of support requirements— especially backups!

Q20. What are the key factors for implementing key system management processes (i.e., Production Acceptance or Change Management)?

A20. There are two primary factors. The first is to get *commitment* and *buy-in* from all levels of the organization. The second is to have centralized ownership via the Production Services organization.

Q21. How can I give my junior, yet promising staff, the proper career development path?

A21. There is a huge gap between junior staff and senior personnel. IT needs to design a Production Services organization that allows junior staff the opportunity to excel to the next level, whether it is technical, nontechnical or management. The PS organization is designed to be a breeding ground for future IT superstars by providing the appropriate functions (see Chapter 4).

Q22. We desperately need to implement a few system management processes. Besides documenting, marketing, and selling these much needed processes to the staff, what else can we do to ensure 100 percent compliance?

A22. The primary way to ensure 100 percent *buy-in* and *commitment* is to hold an Infrastructure Planning and Development workshop (see Chapter 3 for further details).

Summary

This chapter presented some of the most frequently asked questions we receive from infrastructure managers and staff during our workshops, assessments, and consulting activities. In reading through these inquiries, you can see that a few common threads emerge. These threads include the need for executive support for budgeting resources, the need to implement the mainframe disciplines of reliability, availability, and serviceability without the inherent inefficiencies, and the need to focus on Change Management, Problem Management, and Production Acceptance as a means to provide world class stability to any operating environment.

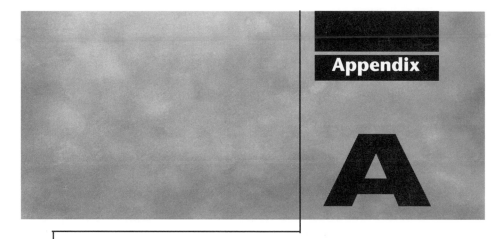

Production Services Job Descriptions

Production Services Management Position

Job Title: Director, Production Services
Dept. Name: Information Technology
Reports To: VP, Enterprise Infrastructure Services

Overall Responsibilities

Responsibilities include managing the functions of Service Level Agreements (SLA)/Metrics Management, Asset Management (operational—not financial) and Process ownership of Production Acceptance and Change Management. The function provides second-level production/ Technical Support and is also responsible for production integrity by acting as the production "gatekeeper."

Specific Responsibilities

- Initiate, develop, implement, and manage a Production Acceptance and Change Management process
- Educate internal customers on the "process" and develop the details and supporting materials needed to move forward with implementation
- Identify a pilot initiative and establish a Production Acceptance Team
- Research, recommend, and implement automated methods to facilitate and control processes
- Produce, route, and provide guidance with a Production Acceptance Questionnaire and kick off formal Production Acceptance meetings and team activities
- Interface with all other IT functions and internal customers of IT
  - Help Desk
  - Systems Administration and Technical Support
  - Networking
  - Database Administration
  - Desktop Support
  - Applications Development, etc.
- Chair the weekly Change Management meeting
- Develop and maintain documentation of detailed processes
- Facilitate all weekly communication
- Identify and document scope of production. Documenting the scope of production will entail sketching the Technical Center's network and system elements, identifying those components within the environment that will be subject to this process and working together with IT management to define what "production" means to your company
- Maintain documentation

Qualifications

- Strong skill set in process-oriented IT functions. Specifically, Change Management & Production Acceptance
- B.S. degree in Operations Management/Research, Business, Computer Science or equivalent experience
- Ability to interact and handle complex issues with users
- Ability to achieve consensus and maintain diplomacy with firmness
- Ability to organize, lead, and be effective with all levels of technical and nontechnical individuals and groups
- Ability to work effectively with users while providing a high standard of customer service

Production Services Staff Position

Job Title: Senior Process Engineer
Dept. Name: Information Technology
Reports To: Director, Production Services

Overall Responsibilities

Responsibilities include developing, implementing, and maintaining the full range of enterprise-wide infrastructure processes. These include, but are not limited to, Change Management, Production Acceptance, Capacity Planning, and Business Continuity. This position also provides second-level production support and mentors, and directs some of the activities of junior-level process engineers.

Specific Responsibilities

- Initiate, develop, implement, and manage specific enterprise-wide infrastructure processes
- Identify specific inputs for the process being developed
  - Process objective
  - Process executive sponsor
  - Process owner
  - Process inputs and outputs
  - Process customers and suppliers
- Design service metrics into the process oriented towards customers
- Design process metrics into the process oriented towards suppliers
- Analyze service and process metrics to enable process improvement recommendations
- Design enforcement methods into the process
- Document initial process and all updates

Qualifications

- Strong skill set in process-oriented IT functions
- Strong people skills
- B.S. degree in Operations Management/Research, Business, Computer Science or equivalent experience
- Ability to interact and handle complex issues with customers and suppliers
- Ability to achieve consensus and maintain diplomacy with firmness
- Ability to organize, lead, and be effective with all levels of technical and nontechnical individuals and groups
- Ability to analyze large amounts of metric data to identify trends, patterns, and relationships

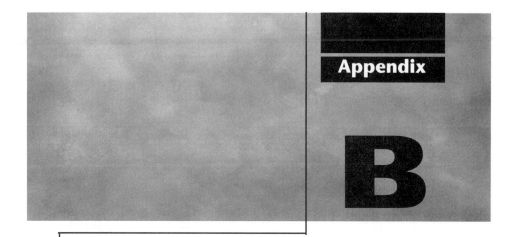

Issues from Workshop

We have facilitated dozens of IT planning and development workshops. After identifying thousands of issues, eighty-three of those issues were reoccurring. In Table B–1, we have categorized these issues, many of which fell into multiple categories. Of the 83 issues, we felt that 32 could be addressed by a PS function.

Table B-1 Issues Likely to be Solved Using a PS Function

#	Description of Issue
1	Three levels of Technical Support (Systems Administration) not defined
2	Difficult for staff to learn new technologies—preoccupied with daily 'fire-fighting drills"
3	Tactical, not strategic, approach
4	IT shops are organizing based on particular technologies (i.e., Mainframe, AS400, NT, UNIX, etc.)
5	Irrational organization structure—responsibility without accountability
6	Two separate Infrastructure Support groups causing combative (power struggle), ineffective, inefficient, inter-group chasm between Infrastructure Development and Production Support
7	Duplicate Systems Administration functions
8	Database Administration has been restructured many times, yet there is still a lot of political infighting
9	Business liaison model should not be eliminated from customer perspective
10	High complexity in the organization structure
11	International technical resources do not report into centralized IT
12	Reinventing the wheel—wasted costs
13	LAN support is split between multiple organizations
14	Lack of a process to market and sell IT services
15	Lack of a Production Acceptance process for client-server applications
16	Lack of a Storage Management process
17	Lack of defined metrics for measuring the effectiveness of IT
18	Need a balance between standards and flexibility
19	Lack of a process to gauge customer productivity
20	Lack of definition of what is mission critical and levels of importance to the business—prioritize
21	Lack of a software version control and code migration process

#	Description of Issue
22	Lack of an Asset Management process
23	Lack of a Capacity Planning process
24	Lack of Configuration Management, in both hardware and software configurations
25	Increased costs for maintenance and upgrades for software to keep software in synch with changing business and technology
26	Technical staff input not used in key decision making throughout IT
27	IT focused on high visibility projects vs. infrastructure planning—thus a separate structure focuses on Production Support
28	Lack of management resources
29	IT management and technical leads are not effectively managing customer expectations
30	Need better communication of standards
31	Lack of communication about decision making at the management level
32	Lack of RAS in production environment
33	Lack of coordination between end-users and support groups
34	Unclear centralized ownership along with scattered responsibilities of technology and process, i.e., Change Management, Production Acceptance, and Problem Management
35	No internal QA process for IT
36	Too many technologies deployed that cannot be efficiently supported
37	Informal Level 2 support structure
38	Lack of senior resources to mentor lower level Technical Support
39	Inability to pool technical resources for specific projects
40	Lack of a Production Control function (Production QA, second-level Systems Administration, process ownership, production gatekeeper, etc.)
41	Lack of an effective enterprise-wide Change Management/Control process
42	Lack of coordinated responses to problems with appropriate escalation or inability to respond
43	Lack of a Business Continuity process

#	Description of Issue
44	Lack of service levels between Infrastructure Services and Applications Development and between IT and Customers
45	Recruiting, retaining, training, mentoring technical resources is difficult; career development is limited
46	Not enough staff to cover all support requirements
47	Lack of enterprise-wide system management and monitoring tools or they're not fully implemented
48	Enterprise-wide Change Control notification process ineffective
49	Lack of clear roles and responsibilities throughout the enterprise
50	Poor communication within the organization on all levels; barriers/walls between groups
51	Help Desk cannot support all technologies they are responsible for
52	Lack of Hardware Management
53	Lack of respect for IT from customer base
54	Meetings—inefficient, too many, difficult to coordinate, often changed, lack of respect for attendance, punctuality, preparation
55	Customer driving technology decisions more than they should
56	IT not seen as a strategic business partner
57	Customers circumvent call process (call who they know, or who will give them the answer they want)
58	Business liaison interface with Infrastructure Support (IT) needs to be more integrated— they promise customers more than IT can deliver
59	Ineffective Problem Management or lack thereof
60	Lack of testing or preproduction environment
61	Need to do a better job of getting the technical resources aligned with the business drivers and requirements
62	Lack of mission and goals of IT as a whole, and the communication of goals and mission
63	Multiple Help Desks—no integration of the corporate with the local Help Desks
64	Split Network Support functions

#	Description of Issue
65	Ineffective project management and lack of resources
66	Lack of a Tape Librarian function
67	Lack of a process to benchmark services
68	Lack of centralized, empowered project management methodology/process
69	Help Desk provides inadequate and/or incorrect information or problem tickets
70	Unclear decision making process, inputs, parameters
71	Philosophy is to say "yes" to customer regardless of their demands; customer perception is the inverse—more common
72	Over reliance on consultants
73	Need "all-IT" meetings on a regular basis
74	Lack of a security policy and staff to manage security
75	The centralized IT group is perceived to be in a glass house/ivory tower environment
76	Lack of standards and adherence to standards throughout the infrastructure—the enterprise
77	Lack of an effective Architecture/Planning function for designing the proper infrastructure
78	Lack of a proper process with curriculum to transition and mentor staff; the consequence is a lack of an effective technical career development path
79	Lack of strategic marketing/selling of IT services
80	Ineffective global coordination
81	Lack of internal and external SLAs
82	Lack of a Disaster Recovery process
83	Multiple support groups, roles and responsibilities unclear for customers; i.e., desktop hardware group, desktop software group, and desktop project group

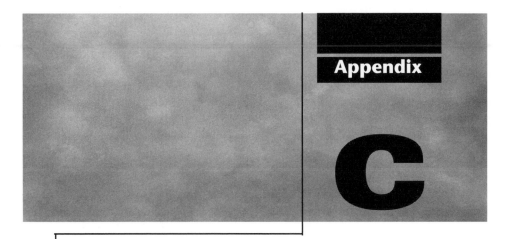

Description of Issues from Workshop

Data from IT Planning and Development Workshop

The data below is comprised of the issues that were highlighted from dozens of our IT planning and development workshops. The participants engaged in a typical brainstorming session and articulated the issues within their IT organization.

Issue

Executive management is always threatening to outsource.

We have seen very few outsourcing partnerships work when organizations outsource their entire infrastructure especially if it's unstable. Selective outsourcing of key, well-running functions (e.g., Help Desk, etc.) have proven to be effective. We have been asked to come in and resolve conflict between outsourcing vendors and their customers throughout the world—we mention no names, but they are some of the biggest in the industry. The impact of outsourcing an unstable environment is:

- Higher IT costs—outsourcing does not save you money
- Frustrated users become even more irritated because IT has introduced another layer of bureaucracy
- Twice the headaches for IT

Solution

It will definitely cost your company more in the long haul. Can outsourcing companies effectively manage network computing environments? We do not believe they can. The mainframe environment is fairly straightforward—servers all over the net are another ballgame! If you have a stable legacy environment, then outsourcing may make sense (e.g., allows you to focus on the latest technology, such as network computing, once again), as long as cost is not the primary reason. To summarize; if you turn over a well-run legacy environment, it can be promising—but if you turn over your unmanageable network computing enterprise, then you will receive twice the trouble in return.

Issue

Our IT organization is always focusing on high visibility projects versus infrastructure planning.

This is a common problem in most IT shops. Executive management has very little choice but to focus on high visibility projects. It would be a career limiting move if they did not. We are not saying they should not, but instead of allocating 100 percent of the budget and resources on high visibility, a 60/40 split would be advantageous to all parties. The infrastructure is begging for attention, so how about starting out with forty percent? Fifty percent would be ideal, but we don't want to push the issue. Infrastructure planning should not be an afterthought—if it is, these projects could very likely fail. The impact from lack of infrastructure planning is:

- High availability will be unattainable
- Frustrated Infrastructure Support staff
- Upset customers mostly due to poor system availability
- Higher costs to maintain the infrastructure

Solution

Infrastructure planning is just as important as systems development and deployment. The only way to ensure proper infrastructure planning is to follow our Ten Commandments (see Chapter 2) and adhere to a Production Acceptance process (see Chapter 5), which ensures involvement, coordination, and that key individuals from the Infrastructure Support and Applications Development organization are addressing proper planning.

Issue

Our Architecture/Planning function does not do a very good job with infrastructure development.

Since the early 1990s, the infrastructure architecture/planning function has been the responsibility of senior architects. These architects typically report to the Chief Information Officer (CIO). Herein lies the problem. In the 1960s, 1970s, and 1980s, senior Technical Support personnel who reported into the infrastructure organization performed this function. Who can build a better infrastructure then those who live in the trenches every day? Unfortunately, ever since client-server was born, this function was transitioned into the hands of the architects. It was delegated to the architects for several reasons:

- Architects have a global view of infrastructure requirements
- Senior technical staff are too busy resolving daily production problems
- Architects would have executive level focus to acquire budget and resources to address the many infrastructure issues we highlight throughout this book

The impact of not having an effective architecture/planning function to build the proper infrastructure is:

- Lack of enterprise-wide technology solutions
- Lack of standards
- Senior technical staff with poor morale—they do not want to spend all their time in a reactive/problem resolution mode
- The proper focus is not given to the infrastructure

Solution

Bring this function back down to the trenches. This function should not be reporting to the CIO. We prefer not having a specialized individual handling this function—your senior technicians should be given the bandwidth to handle this function. They certainly have the experience! Follow our Ten Commandments to building the ideal IT environment (see Chapter 2).

Issue

It is difficult for our staff to learn new technologies when they are preoccupied with daily "fire-fighting drills."

This has been a big challenge with every IT organization we have assessed. Technical Support staff (i.e., Systems Administration, Database Administration, and so on) is in a reactive, tactical mode versus the more strategic. Typically, customer initiated, IT related problems are routed directly to senior technical, or in some companies users bypass the Help Desk altogether and go directly to senior personnel. The impact of not addressing this issue is:

- Ineffective use of senior resources
- Lack of technical resources
- Frustrated technical staff
- High staff turnaround

Solution

These highly paid, intelligent individuals are running around in circles resolving the simplest of problems that could be resolved by mid-level staff. These senior technicians should be spending eighty percent of their time designing world class infrastructures by fully implementing and customizing system management tools, and analyzing the latest and greatest technology. Technology is changing daily. System management planning/ analysis is imperative in implementing more of an automated data center environment. Thus, the organization loses out on opportunities to optimize the use of new technologies.

IT infrastructure organizations need to establish three levels of support to better support mission-critical systems. The objective is to handle as many of the tactical issues/problems with Level 1 and Level 2 Technical Support staff to free up Level 3 senior staff.

Issue

There is a lot of political infighting and poor communication between our Applications Development organization and Infrastructure Support staff.

Businesses have enough competition outside the business without having it inside as well. Of all the battles inside IT, none are worse than those between Applications Development and the Infrastructure Services Organization. Even when development and support were centralized under one organization, there was always finger pointing. The charter for Applications Development is to design, develop, and deploy systems into production as quickly as possible. The charter for Infrastructure Support is to ensure proper standards, guidelines, and QA testing are followed, and thorough documentation is provided. Most of the issues arise around deployment and support of mission-critical applications. Another area where developers and Operations support staff did not see eye-to-eye was performing Systems Administration functions (i.e., backups, restores) of development servers. Infrastructure Support staff wants development staff to have limited access to their servers, and development staff usually wants full access. There are many issues of this nature.

The impact is:

- Constant political infighting
- Lack of communication
- Frustrated IT staff and customers
- Unstable systems
- Wasted system management efforts

Solution

To keep your Infrastructure Support group and your Applications Development staff away from each other's throats, IT needs to implement a Production Acceptance process (see Chapter 5) for deploying and supporting mission-critical applications into production. The primary objective of the Production Acceptance process is to improve communication between these two organizations.

To address other non-production issues (i.e., Systems Administration of development or test servers) we recommend implementing an internal SLA.

Issue

Our IT department does not have enough resources.

This is a common theme throughout IT. As long as your Infrastructure Support functions are constantly in a reactive mode, you will NEVER have enough resources. The impact of this issue is:

- Poor morale
- Poor communication
- Not enough time to properly implement enterprise-wide systems management solutions
- Barriers and walls between groups
- Lack of time to internally breed technical resources
- Lack of time to implement the proper processes to streamline and automate much of the production environment

Solution

Asking for additional resources is not always the solution. The solution is to free up your senior technical resources so they can build a stable infrastructure. As mentioned previously, once the organization is structured properly, senior technical staff will also have the opportunity to train junior and mid-level staff.

Issue

Every time we acquire a new company with a different technology, we scramble to restructure the organization to support a new technology.

IT shops are too busy organizing based on particular technologies (i.e. Mainframe, AS400, NT, UNIX, and so on). Each time a new technology is introduced into the infrastructure, whether it is to support a new business system or from a corporate acquisition, the results are usually the same. A new organization will sprout up to support it. Each one of these organizations are going to do what they see fit to support their line of business. The impact of this issue is:

- Poor morale
- Poor communication
- Resources become scarce
- Lack of enterprise-wide systems management planning
- Barriers and walls between groups

Solution

It is a necessity for organizations to have specific technical expertise to support a particular technology, but all these disparate groups should report to one Infrastructure Services Organization. This Technical Support organization can then address enterprise-wide solutions versus point solutions.

Issue

We have multiple support groups; roles and responsibilities are unclear for our customers (i.e., desktop hardware group, desktop software group, and desktop project group).

Sometimes there is a separate group responsible for desktop hardware and another for software. There is also a separate group responsible for desktop projects. If this is confusing for you, think about the poor computer-illiterate customer. The impact is:

- It is difficult for the Help Desk to determine who to call for problems
- IT loses credibility
- Customers become frustrated and unproductive

Solution

IT needs to structure the organization using our Ten Commandments as guidelines (see Chapter 2 for further details). There should be a single point of contact for the customer.

Issue

Our production environment is unstable.

The two biggest reasons are: the organization is not structured properly to support mission-critical and system management processes (disciplines) are missing or ineffective. Organization, people and process initiatives are usually placed on the back burner because most of the resources and budget are focused toward new systems development. Other reasons could be:

- Lack of centralized ownership and accountability for key processes
- Lack of focus
- Poor Facilities Management
- Lack of standards
- Poor technology architecture
- Lack of an infrastructure QA methodology

IT needs to have one QA methodology for turning over new code into production and one for deploying new systems to the Infrastructure Services Organization (see Chapter 5). Most IT organizations have a QA process to migrate new code into production. Very few organizations, however, have an overall QA methodology to ensure infrastructure requirements are addressed prior to transitioning systems into production.

The impact is:

- High availability will be unattainable
- Lack of effective system management solutions
- The environment is reactive in nature
- Higher costs

- An unstable production environment
- Poor morale

Solution

Effectively supporting mission-critical applications, regardless of the platform and paradigm, is extremely difficult. It is crucial to take the best practices from the legacy environment along with a focus on customer service to build a world class production environment. The data center has always stood for high availability and security supported by a very disciplined staff. The staff members were bred in a very disciplined environment—from keeping the facilities spotless to treating data devices as if they were gold. Their lives revolved around the data center 24 hours a day, seven days a week.

Issue

Our Help Desk has no authority.

Without authority, the Help Desk is nothing but a problem router—answer the phone and route the problem. Once it leaves their hands, it goes into Never Never Land. In many companies, the Help Desk organization is structured with the Desktop Services organization or buried with some other group within the infrastructure organization. The impact is:

- Ineffective Problem Management
- Frustrated users
- Inadequate problem resolution

Solution

The Help Desk should always be structured at the enterprise level, reporting directly to the Vice President of Infrastructure with *clear* ownership of the Problem Management process.

Issue

Our Database Administration organization has been restructured many times, yet there is still a lot of political infighting.

The Database Administration group is one of the most controversial functions in IT. Structuring this group has been a debate since the client-server paradigm was born. In many companies, Database Administration is organized under Applications Development, for others it is Operations support, and for others it is split between the two. The impact is:

- Poor communications
- Problem resolution is not very effective
- Duplication of efforts

Solution

There should be one centralized Database Administration function structure reporting into the infrastructure organization.

Issue

Our Problem Management process is ineffective.

Regardless of how well designed its processes, or how smoothly running its Operations are, even a world class infrastructure will occasionally miss its targeted levels of service. The discipline that deals with the handling of these occurrences is called Problem Management. Problem Management is a process to identify, log, track, resolve, and analyze problems impacting IT Services. Without an effective Problem Management process, the impact is:

- Uncoordinated responses to problems
- High availability becomes an unattainable goal

- Lack of problem ownership and accountability
- People are tied up in priorities—they do not have the time to document the problems/issues
- Lack of follow-up
- Problems get lost—no tracking
- There is a lack of information
- Lack of root cause analysis
- Lack of closed-loop feedback
- Level 2 analysts not putting in detailed description of how they resolved the problem
- Many of the groups provide no feedback on problems being worked

Solution

Eventually customers will circumvent the Help Desk and call whom they know, or who will give them the answer they want. An ineffective Problem Management process is a common problem. Problem Management is one of the most critical processes and disciplines within IT. There are eleven steps to developing the proper Problem Management process:

- Select an executive sponsor
- Assign a process owner
- Assemble a cross functional team
- Identify and prioritize requirements
- Establish a priority and escalation scheme
- Identify alternative call tracking tools
- Negotiate service levels
- Develop service and process metrics
- Design the call handling process; evaluate, select, and implement the call tracking tool
- Review metrics to continually improve the process

For further details on implementing a robust Problem Management process, see our book titled *IT Systems Management* by Rich Schiesser.

Issue

We need a balance between standards and flexibility. We don't want to be labeled "slow."

A common problem is determining how much discipline (standards, processes, and procedures) is just the right amount. As noted in our list of Ten Commandments (see Chapter 2), never trash mainframe disciplines (standards and processes) but work to keep the bureaucracy out as you are designing these disciplines. The impact of not having standards is:

- Higher costs to IT
- Integration of technologies is difficult
- Wasted resources
- Duplication of efforts

Solution

A good rule of thumb is to design standards that are minimal and sufficient. There are no alternatives here. Standards and processes are essential.

Issue

We have two separate Infrastructure Services groups causing a combative (power struggle), ineffective, inefficient, inter-group chasm between infrastructure development and Infrastructure Support.

In several instances, we have found infrastructure organizations split between production support and infrastructure development. Trying to separate projects and support is very difficult. Technical staff gets pulled off of support for new project implementations—technicians prefer working on new projects. The impact is:

- Staff not implementing new projects have a difficult time supporting them
- Production support not receiving the recognition, as does the staff working on new projects, but when problems occur they are the ones that work the overtime
- Difficult to designate a senior technician for production support only

Solution

There should only be one enterprise-wide IT infrastructure organization. The staff may be decentralized and located all across the globe, but there needs to be a centralized organization with the authority to establish guidelines, standards, and processes to which all adhere.

Issue

We do not have a career development plan.

Organizations today do not intentionally or systematically breed senior technical staff. Technologists are hired and are usually permanently affixed into their current position. Very few companies have a technical or management career path. The impact is:

- Technical resources are scarce
- Loss of opportunity to grow internal IT staff
- Poor morale

Solution

Having the proper career path was one of those areas that management always talked about, but rarely was there a formal plan in place with the staff. In many IT shops, management would allow their technical staff to attend training, but rarely did management address the big picture of what happens to:

- Technical staff that would like to venture into management
- Nontechnical staff who want to dabble in technology
- Junior staff who want the opportunity to work with senior personnel for some hands-on training

The root cause of these issues starts with the organizational structure. There should be three levels of support so that junior, mid-level, and senior technical staffs are working together to resolve production problems. The organization should also be structured with a PS group, whose primary focus is the design, implementation, and maintenance of processes. Another function of this group should be used as second-level support.

Issue

Our Change Management process is ineffective.

Change Management is one of the oldest and most important of all systems management disciplines. You might think that, with so many years to refine this process and grow aware of its importance, Change Management would be widely used, well designed, properly implemented, effectively executed, and have little room for improvement. Surprisingly, in the eyes of many executives, just the reverse is true. The problems are:

- Not all changes are logged
- Changes not thoroughly tested
- Lack of enforcement
- Lack of effective method for communicating within IT
- Coordination within the groups is poor—only the person attending the change meetings is aware of the events; on many occasions the information is not disseminated throughout the organization

- Lack of centralized ownership
- Change Management is not effective; in some instances, changes are being made on the production servers without coordination or communication
- Lack of approval policy
- Hard copies of *changes* kept in file cabinets
- On many occasions, notification is made to all after the fact
- Managers and directors required to sign a hard copy of every change
- Current process is the only form for notification
- The process is bureaucratic and not user-friendly

There are several different flavors of Change Management. Change Management is a process that coordinates any change that can potentially impact the operational production environment. In many shops, the staff bypasses this process. This process should be part of your overall infrastructure QA methodology. The impact of not having an effective Change Management process is:

- High availability will be unattainable due to a very unstable production environment
- Problem determination will be very difficult and time consuming

Solution

An effective Change Management process is crucial to attaining high availability. There are 13 steps involved in designing a robust Change Management process. Our book entitled *IT Systems Management* by Rich Schiesser describes these steps:

1. Identify an executive sponsor.
2. Assign a process owner.
3. Select a cross functional process design team.
4. Arrange for meetings of the cross-functional process design team.
5. Establish roles and responsibilities for members supporting the design team.
6. Identify the benefits of a Change Management process.

7. If change metrics exist, collect and analyze them; if not, set up a process to do so.

8. Identify and prioritize requirements.

9. Develop definitions of key terms.

10. Design the initial Change Management process.

11. Develop policy statements.

12. Develop a charter for a Change Review Board (CRB).

13. Use the CRB to continually refine and improve the Change Management process.

Issue

There is a lack of coordination between end-users, development organizations, and support groups for supporting our mission-critical systems.

Effective communication practices have always been an issue in data processing, but when client-server came along, it became worse. Client-server changed the entire playing field. Communication became more difficult than ever because of the speed of change. Development efforts, which took years and were generally centralized under one, became a practice of the past. Systems were being developed in weeks and months all over the world—even in third world countries. The impact of not effectively coordinating and communicating support requirements for mission-critical systems is:

- Poor communication
- Unstable systems
- Duplication of efforts

Solution

To address this communication problem, we developed the Production Acceptance process. The reason we developed this process was because there is very little communication or coordination between Applications

Development, Infrastructure Support, and end-users. In this day and age, when technology is moving at the speed of light, the perception is that any process to coordinate efforts will slow down system deployment. The Production Acceptance process is streamlined and nonbureaucratic. Its primary objective is to improve communication between these organizations (see Chapter 5).

Issue

Our LAN support is split between multiple organizations.

It is vital to have local or regional Technical Support. We do not have a problem with this, but we do have a problem with every location establishing its own standards for technology. The impact of this is:

- Wasted costs to IT
- Confusion for the people who use and staff the Help Desk
- Duplication of system management efforts
- Confusion for the end-users

Solution

LAN support staff can be decentralized, but there should be one owner for this function worldwide. The goal should be to have as few point solutions as possible. To effectively manage IT, there needs to be enterprise-wide standards.

Issue

There is a lack of respect from our customer base towards our IT organization.

There are many reasons for this, including:

- Unsatisfactory service levels
- Poor system availability
- Lack of customer service focus
- Complexity within the IT organization
- Poor customer support
- Perception of bureaucracy and laggardness
- IT is too costly
- Poor communication
- Lack of marketing and selling of IT Services

One of the biggest reasons is that IT does a poor job of communicating with its customers. When you do not effectively communicate with your customers, the perception they have of IT will always be negative. The impact is:

- Lack of respect for IT
- Irate users
- Cries to outsource IT

Solution

IT should follow all Ten Commandments for building the ideal IT Organization (see Chapter 2). One of the Ten Commandments highlights the need to communicate with customers via a process. Weekly meetings will not improve communication and coordination. A process has to spearhead effective communication practices!

Issue

Our organization seems very complex.

In many IT shops, we found their organizational structures to be extremely complex. The impact is:

- Difficult to implement and administer processes
- Poor communication
- Problem Management is not effective
- Confusion for your customers
- Wasted resources

Solution

IT must do everything possible to keep things simple for its staff, and more importantly for its customers. Structure the infrastructure organization into two separate support functions—one for mission-critical and the other for non-mission-critical (see Chapter 2) functions. Everything cannot possibly be mission critical (24×7 support). With today's budget constraints, IT needs to clearly define their scope of production and structure itself appropriately. Teach the staff that a production system is a production system is a production system, and if it falls under the mission critical category, then prioritize accordingly. IT should always structure the organization to distinguish mission-critical and non-mission-critical structure for technology's sake.

Issue

We need "all-IT" meetings on a regular basis.

Downward communication is a huge issue in IT because of:

- The pace of technology
- New systems deployment

- Numerous projects/initiatives
- The reactive nature of the organization

Solution

Your IT organization needs to have quarterly all-hands meetings.

Issue

We have an irrational organization structure—responsibility without accountability.

Processes are being designed and developed by a special task force residing outside of the Infrastructure Services Organization and then turned over to Operations without centralized ownership and accountability. Although Operations staff were probably involved in the design of these processes, there is still a lack of ownership. Herein lies the problem. The impact of responsibility without accountability is:

- Ineffective processes
- Wasted IT costs
- Frustrated staff
- Wasted resources
- Duplication of effort and overlap throughout the entire organization
- Loss of IT credibility
- Political infighting
- Sporadic applications unavailability
- Lack of enterprise-wide solutions
- Groups have their own versions of these processes within the IT organization

Solution

Processes require centralized ownership and accountability. The best way to ensure effective processes is to let people in the trenches design them and maintain them. There must be a centralized (i.e., PS) group that designs, develops, and manages key enterprise-wide processes (i.e., Change Management, Problem Management, Production Acceptance, and so on). Accountability is essential. A special task force should NEVER develop processes. It should be designed and developed from staff that actually works with it daily. If processes are designed and maintained by the same group, *buy-in* (which is key to success) becomes a foregone conclusion.

Issue

There's an overreliance on consultants in our shop.

This is a huge issue. Unfortunately, not too much can be done about it—especially if IT is short on resources and key systems need to be developed quickly for business reasons. The impact is:

- Dependency on consultants
- Higher costs to IT
- Frustrated staff
- Knowledge transfer due to poor documentation

Solution

IT needs to ensure these systems are thoroughly documented. The best way of ensuring this becomes a reality is to make sure each new production system or major revision to existing systems goes through a Production Acceptance process.

Issue

Roles and responsibilities not clearly defined.

Everyone is responsible for everything but rarely does someone own anything. This is a common theme throughout IT. The impact is:

- Political infighting
- Loss of IT credibility
- Duplication of efforts and overlap throughout the entire organization
- Wasted resources
- Higher costs for IT

Solution

Network computing has made the lines between organizations very blurry. At the very least, there needs to be a simple organizational structure with associated job descriptions for every function. IT also needs to ensure compliance with a Production Acceptance process, which spells out everyone's roles and responsibilities by application (who does what to whom and when) for each and every mission-critical system.

Issue

Our centralized IT group is perceived to be in a glass house/ ivory tower environment.

This perception of the centralized IT group has always been that of a very slow, bureaucratic, and costly organization. The impact is

- Customers will look elsewhere for services
- Perception will eventually become a reality
- Higher costs to the company

- Interoperability or integration will become difficult
- The group becomes a potential outsourcing target

Solution

Although it will not be easy, there are several steps that IT needs to take in order to change this perception (for further details see our book entitled *Managing IT as an Investment*). IT needs to:

- Manage technology as a *strategic asset* rather than as a cost center
- *Partner* with the business and become part of the business rather than being apart from the business
- Build a culture based on *shared values*
- Recognize and *communicate value* to the enterprise

As long as IT is perceived to be slow and bureaucratic, the customer will always drive technology decisions more than they should.

Issue

There is a lack of enterprise-wide, system management tools.

It is not so much that there is a lack of system management tools; it's the lack of enterprise-wide system management planning. Most companies have spent hundreds of thousands—if not millions—of dollars on system management tools. The problem is they are not fully implemented in most companies. No one has the time to provide the proper enterprise-wide, system management solutions. The impact is:

- Manual intervention
- Wasted costs
- Occasional glitches
- Wasted technical resources
- High availability cannot be attained
- Point solutions versus enterprise solutions

IT infrastructure organizations need to structure to focus on cost-effectively supporting mission-critical systems and keep customer service included in their planning efforts (see Chapter 4).

Issue

Our international Infrastructure Services Organization implements whatever solutions make sense for their region and nobody looks at the big integration picture.

Global coordination is always challenging, especially when remote organizations do not report into centralized IT Departments. Remote locations do what is best for their community and rarely look at the big picture. The impact is:

- Poor communication
- Frustration for IT staff
- Duplication of efforts
- Poor enterprise-wide planning
- Wasted technical resources
- An enterprise that's difficult/impossible to cost-effectively manage

Solution

At the very least, there should be centralized control at the enterprise level of infrastructure standards and systems management processes.

Issue

We do a horrible job of marketing our service offerings.

The process of marketing and selling IT services still is not being done effectively, and in many shops is not being practiced at all. Without the proper focus, the impact is:

- Poor relationships with your internal customers
- Customers who don't know which direction to turn for IT services
- Customers who look outside the company for support
- IT is still looked upon as only a support function versus a strategic business partner

Solution

IT first has to identify its customers, then determine the value and price of the product and service offerings, and finally establish a delivery vehicle to market these services. This needs to be a full time job function—not something you do on a part-time basis. The function of marketing and selling needs to be part of each and every manager's responsibility. No one has the time, but this can no longer be an excuse. As the leader of IT, the CIO must take responsibility to market IT's services to the enterprise. IT still has a terrible image in most companies and network computing has made things worse. Customers complain about the lack of attention. This perception needs to go away once and for all. In the era of outsourcing, any IT organization is in competition with other providers that might provide this service better, cheaper, and more efficiently to the enterprise. IT professionals need to start today by thoroughly documenting their services and the associated costs for these services.

Issue

We have multiple Help Desks—there is no integration of the corporate function with the local Help Desks.

This has been an issue for decades. In many companies, each division or business unit is managed autonomously and has their own Help Desk function to provide specialized services to their customers. We do not have an issue with this, but we do have an issue with each one of these local or regional Help Desks designing their own Problem Management process or purchasing whatever tool they desire to effectively manage problems. The impact is:

- Duplication of efforts
- Confusion for end-users
- Multiple owners or no ownership of problems/issues
- Higher costs to the corporation

Solution

At the very least, there should be one enterprise-wide, Problem Management process. It makes sense to have regional Help Desks and, if at all possible, one enterprise-wide solution to manage trouble tickets.

Issue

We don't have a production gatekeeper function.

Systems are being developed in weeks and months, and it seems like applications need to be in production yesterday. Can anyone slow it down? Not really, but there can be an infrastructure QA process to ensure production integrity.

During the mainframe era, this function was called Production Control. When client-server was born, most IT organizations made this function obsolete solely because it was related to mainframe computing. The perception of this function was that it was a slow, bureaucratic, and non-customer service oriented function. Without it, the impact is:

- Poor system availability
- Lack of second-level support
- Lack of documentation
- Lack of a proper career development path for Technical Support staff
- Lack of centralized ownership and accountability for key enterprise-wide processes

Solution

Every IT organization implementing and supporting mission-critical systems needs to implement a PS function. Although the perception may have been a reality, why trash the entire function? The idea is to streamline and bring it back (see Chapter 1).

Issue

We have no way to compare our costs with other IT organizations.

Much can be said for the benefits of benchmarking. Its main purpose is to provide an exemplar—a high *watermark*, so to speak, after which you look to model your specific functional area or business. Two challenges exist with a successful benchmarking exercise. The first challenge is to effectively collect and organize benchmark data so you are making an *apples-to-apples* comparison of the operations you are studying. Developing an outline of the information you are trying to gather, and developing an associated questionnaire to help you in your efforts to be consistent in your fact collection, can more easily facilitate this. The second challenge is finding a business, similar to your business, which truly has what is considered a *benchmark* operation (see the book by Tony Tardugno entitled *IT Services*, for addition information). The impact is that management can continue threatening to outsource IT.

Solution

Implementing a benchmarking process, and applying a focused approach while retaining primary process steps, is key to successful benchmarking. The primary steps are:

- Establishing the reason to benchmark
- Developing an understanding of the current environment's needs
- Identifying appropriate target companies
- Developing a methodology of collecting information
- Committing to a plan of utilizing the information collected

Note: For more details, see our book entitled *IT Services* by Tony Tardugno.

Issue

We don't have a formal Tape Librarian function.

Many of the smaller IT organizations are not taking this function seriously. Without this function, the impact is:

- Data integrity is compromised
- Minimum Disaster Recovery requirements are nonexistent
- Loss of data

Solution

The management of data will *always* be a very critical function. Many IT organizations disregard the tape librarian function as a cost reduction exercise. Put it back in! It's Data Processing 101—it is not even up for discussion!

Issue

Lack of defined metrics for measuring the effectiveness of IT.

Performance metrics are nonexistent in just about every IT shop we visit. That old saying holds true here—if you cannot measure it, there is no way you can manage it effectively. The impact of not having metrics is:

- You cannot effectively manage the infrastructure

Solution

It is important to establish internal metrics for each area of the operations, as well as quarterly or semiannual ratings, to compare the results based on cost and performance efficiencies.

Issue

There is a lack of standards and adherence to standards throughout the infrastructure.

With the pace of change and technology in IT, standards are sometimes overlooked. The impact is:

- Higher costs to the company
- Integration issues are enormous

Solution

IT organizations should strive for enterprise-wide standards, such as:

- Global Standard Desktop Operating System
- Global Standard Desktop Application Suite
- Global Standard Server Operating System

- Global Standard Messaging and Collaboration Platform
- Global Standard Remote Access
- Global Standard Application Distribution Platform
- Global Standard Data Backup
- Global Standard Virus Scanning
- Global Standard Server Hardware
- Global Standard Data Backup
- Global Standard Monitoring
- Global Standard Development Database
- Global Standard Development Methods and Tools
- Global Standard Desktop Hardware
- Global Standard Network

Issue

We do not have a business continuity process.

Before 9/11, very few IT organizations invested time or resources in developing a business continuity plan. Times have changed!

Business continuity is a proactive approach to ensure the continuous operation of critical business systems in the event of widespread or localized disasters to an infrastructure environment. The impact of not having a business continuity process is:

- Lack of access or compromise of integrity of a company's critical data
- Downtime of a company's mission-critical systems for days or weeks could cost millions of dollars in lost revenue and untold losses in reputation.

Solution

A comprehensive business continuity plan will ensure continuous access to, and operation of, critical business systems. The plan needs to be well designed, thoroughly tested, and kept up to date. A robust business continuity process will include business impact analysis, contingency planning, and Disaster Recovery.

Business impact analysis identifies the financial and operational impact of critical business processes not being available over increasing periods of time. Critical dependencies of these systems are also identified. Contingency planning proposes alternative recovery strategies based on the likelihood of given disaster scenarios. Disaster Recovery is a detailed plan to execute the recovery strategy appropriate for a given event.

For further details on implementing a robust business continuity and Disaster Recovery process, see our book entitled *IT Systems Management* by Rich Schiesser.

Issue

Our Applications Development organization throws its newly developed systems over the wall to Operations.

Very few IT organizations have a process that coordinates the efforts between Applications Development and Operations to successfully transition and deploy a system into production. If they do have such a process, it's weighted more towards the Applications Development requirements than infrastructure requirements.

Production Acceptance is a process that engages Applications/Systems Development and Infrastructure Support functions early on to effectively deploy and support all systems in production. The majority of IT organizations do not have a Production Acceptance process. The impact of this is:

- High availability is unattainable
- Poor communication between IT and its customers
- Production support staff is not sufficiently trained
- Lack of proper documentation
- Roles and responsibilities unclear for supporting mission-critical systems

Solution

IT needs to implement a Production Acceptance process (see Chapter 5). It is the key process for effectively transitioning mission-critical systems from development to production.

Issue

We do not have a strategic security process.

Strategic security is a process designed to safeguard the availability, integrity, and confidentiality of designated data and programs. The impact of not having this process is:

- Unauthorized access, modification, or destruction of critical or sensitive company data

Solution

A strategic security process describes the architecture and policies under which all security related matters are be managed. An effective strategic security program has two important sub-processes supporting it. One process describes how to initiate, approve, and implement new security policies. The other shows how to enforce, monitor, and maintain policies already in existence.

Issue

We do not have a Capacity Planning process.

Capacity Planning is a process for predicting the types, quantities, and timing of critical resource capacities that are needed within an infrastructure to accurately meet forecasted workloads. The impact of not having this process is:

- Inability to supply required resources for new systems
- Inability to sustain performance service levels during peak or growth periods
- Costly and last minute rushing to meet demand for increased capacity

Solution

A rigorous Capacity Planning process accurately forecasts future workloads to enable the proper sizing and timing of required resources. This program also partners IT with its key customers by encouraging meaningful discussions on the number and types of online transactions expected over periods of time.

For further details on implementing a robust Capacity Planning process, see our book titled *IT Systems Management* by Rich Schiesser.

Issue

We have an unclear decision making process, including inputs and parameters.

When managers and their staff are not sure who is responsible for making specific types of decisions, chaos results. Even when the authority for this responsibility is clearly understood, staff can still become confused and impacted by decisions that are:

- Ill-conceived
- Poorly communicated
- Only partially implemented

Solution

Managers and staff alike can benefit from a robust decision making process. Such a process needs to be logically designed, well documented, and widely communicated. Technical decisions need to be based on solid facts and data, and strategic decisions need to support the business goals of the corporation. The result will be a much less chaotic, and more stable, efficient infrastructure.

Issue

We do not have the proper testing or preproduction environment.

One of the most critical requirements to a successfully deployed application is a testing environment that closely mirrors the production environment. The impact of not having this environment is:

- Deploying new systems containing functionality problems
- Installing applications whose response times do not meet service levels
- Delays in deploying new systems
- Loss of credibility of the IT department

Solution

A preproduction testing environment can help in the deploying of new systems by debugging program errors, uncovering functionality flaws, surfacing issues of capacity requirements, and troubleshooting performance problems. It also can provide users with a suitable setting for rigorous acceptance testing. The testing environment should reflect the actual production environment as closely as possible. This includes hardware configurations, software release levels, and simulated loads to stress resource capacity.

Issue

We need to do a better job of getting the technical resources aligned with the business drivers and requirements.

IT is often enamored with technology simply for technology's sake, rather than focusing on the use of technology to solve business problems. The impact of this can be:

- Major expenditures on unused technology
- Loss of competitive advantage
- Resentment of business units toward a unresponsive IT department

Solution

IT management needs to nurture a close, supportive relationship with key business unit customers of IT services. A close partnering of this type can produce a clearer understanding of the true business needs of the customer, and a more practical technical solution to meet these needs.

Issue

There is a lack of mission and goals (and the communication thereof) within IT as a whole.

A surprising number of IT shops do not have clearly defined mission statements or strategic goals. Others may have their missions and goals defined, but fail to effectively communicate them to those needing them the most—the staff responsible for accomplishing these goals. The impact of this is:

- Staff pursuing divergent, sometime opposing, goals
- Conflicting priorities

- Miscommunication to customers
- Loss of morale

Solution

A clear, succinct IT mission statement should define the purpose and direction of that department. The mission must be effectively communicated to all members of IT to ensure uniformity, support, and teamwork. There also needs to be a clear understanding of the goals that support and enact the mission statement. Goals need to be reasonable, measurable, and prioritized with an individual assigned accountability for the successful completion of each goal.

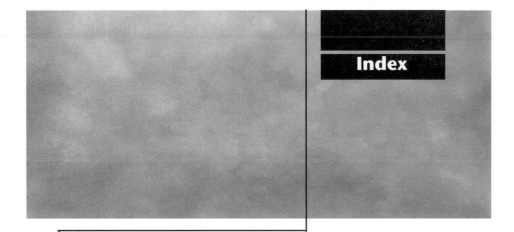

Index

T

tape liberation 2
tape librarian 175
technical support 150–151
    decentralization of 164
    for new technology 154
technology 23, 181
test plans, revision of 80
three-tier support model 19, 63–66
training 18
    in non-mission critical systems 21
    revision of 80

V

value of information technology 28–29
values 29–30

W

wide area networks (WANs) 21
workshops 44–45
    deliverables 46
    issues and resolution categories in 49–59, 142–145
    objectives of 45–46
    post-workshop activities 48
    schedule for 46–47
    See also issues and solutions

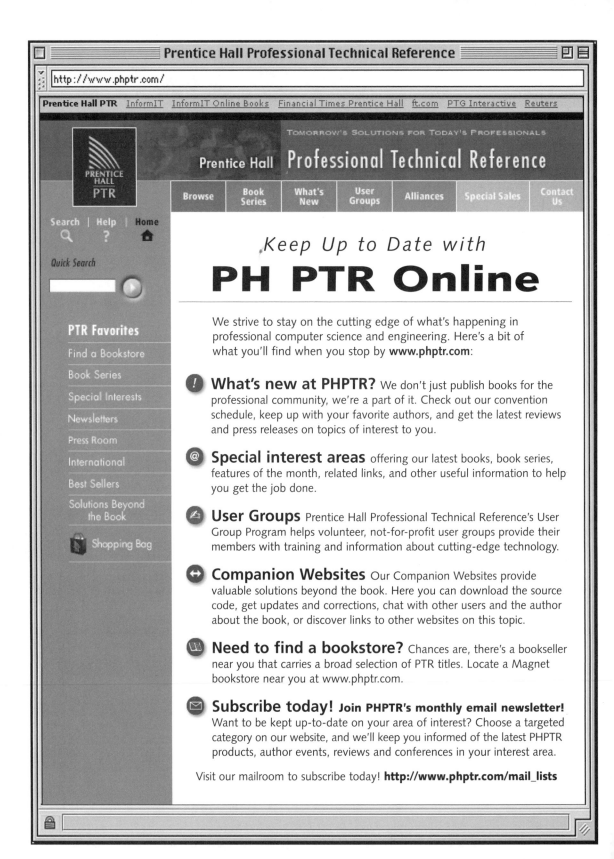